MAYFAIR TO MOSCOW

MOSCOW

CLARE SHERIDAN'S DIARY

1921

Contents

PUBLISHER'S NOTES

Free-spirited Clare Consuelo Sheridan (9 September 1885—31 May 1970) led a remarkable life. Sculptor and writer, and she traveled extensively and wrote of her journeys.

She was also a lover to Charlie Chaplin, and possibly had affairs with the Russian revolutionaries she sculpted while in that country in 1920. She spoke favorably of Trotsky and Lenin (and spoke with them quite a bit) and earned herself a file in the archives of her native England's MI-5 as an anti-British propagandist.

On this visit to Russia, she sculpted most of the top Bolsheviks and more importantly, saw them as people and not political icons. Her conversations with them are fascinating, as they are not the ponderous, didactic discussions of polemicists but just two people talking.

She met and visited with American John Reed in Russia, author of *Ten Days that Shook the World* and with her friend H.G. Wells while he was in that country.

She was a cousin of Winston Churchill, whom she adored despite their widely divergent political views. In a conversation with Trotsky, he said to her:

"I will hold you as a hostage until England makes peace with us."

Clair laughed, "What you are saying humorously is what a British Official told me seriously, only he said it apropos of Winston. As a matter of fact, I'd be proud if I could be of any use in the cause of Peace. But if you said you would shoot me, Winston would only say 'shoot,' which is to my mind the right spirit, and exactly the spirit that prevails among the Bolsheviks."

It was on her year-long trip to America that she kept another journal and had an affair with Charlie Chaplin, of whom she writes much in these pages.

She found Americans to her liking and visited many interesting places in the U.S. and Mexico. Everywhere she went, she was "hunting heads" to sculpt.

She was the guest of many prominent Americans, including Sinclair Lewis, Senator Henry Cabot Lodge, Sam Goldwyn, and more famous people than you could shake a stick at. All of this she relates in her unique voice.

PREFACE

The publication of a diary not meant for publication seems to demand some introduction and explanation. I have always kept a diary, even in comparatively monotonous as in eventful days, but I am not a writer. It is almost with a feeling of apology that I venture to swell the ranks of those who publish their little books after their little visits to Russia. In doing so I do not pretend to present a picture of Russia. I was only in Moscow where portrait work, not politics, was my concern.

What I learnt about Bolshevism and the point of view of its leaders can come from illustrative remarks, often quite casually made, as for instance when I was solemnly asked one day what position Bernard Shaw would hold in the new Labor Cabinet, and they were surprised when I giggled.

There are people in England who are indignant at my sculpting Lenin and Trotsky. There were people in Moscow who were horrified because I had done Winston Churchill and expressed a desire to do D'Annunzio, but as I am before all else a portraitist, it is the psychology of people that interests me, not their politics. I love humanity, with its force and its weakness, its ambitions and fears, its honesty and its lack of scruples, its perfection and deformities.

If I found any of the Bolshevik leaders human, agreeable and even kindly, it is probably because they reacted as all human nature does, to the attitude of mind with which it is met.

If I have any political views in my own country they are certainly not in harmony with the policy of Mr. Lloyd George. Nevertheless I have found myself next to him at dinner and enjoyed our discussions on abstract subjects, never touching politics. It may even be that the Prime Minister equally enjoyed these discussions which gave his mind a rest from the work he was intent upon. It seemed that certain of the Soviet rulers with whom I talked were just as happy and more so), than Mr. Lloyd George, to find some one with whom it was not necessary to pursue the political problem. Especially was this the case with Trotsky whom I found very cultured and companionable, and with whom I hardly at all talked about Revolutions!

Before I started for Russia my cousin, Winston Churchill, came to lunch at my studio, and so also Mr. Ambrose McEvoy (the English portrait painter). A short while ago, just after I had landed in New York, I met McEvoy and he talked to me about that luncheon, and commented on my discretion in not disclosing my acquaintance with the Bolshevik emissaries in London, and never breathing a suggestion of my prospective visit to Russia! On the same occasion we discussed Bolshevism pretty openly. I remember that Winston said Bolshevism was a crocodile, that either you must shoot it, or else make a detour round it so as not to rouse it! But I gathered that immediate attack was the policy he favored. But whatever his views were, I have always loved him as I would a brother, and I have admired him for his undoubted courage and purposefulness; and though I do not always agree with him, we find other subjects of deep interest to us both, to talk about and always he is interesting.

At the time when I was doing his portrait bust, he said to me thoughtfully one day: "Clare! You have the most enviable position in the world—you are a woman, you are an artist, you are free and you have children." He has often said to me: "Do you realize how lucky you are?" I wonder if he is right, that as a woman my talents are the more valuable to me. Certain it is that everything good and interesting and all the things worth while that have come to me have come through my work.

I did not always work, and that is why parts of my diary need explanation, parts in which, owing to a mood or an incident, I have burst out impatiently with criticism of my bringing-up.

One does not readily tell of oneself, especially if one is not self-absorbed. But I have been asked to explain why I became a worker.

Some day, when I am no longer physically strong enough to continue the life of a sculptor, I shall, in the evening of my days, write a book, and it will tell of things from the beginning, and be written with pure sincerity. It will relate and explain many things, and some people will not care to read it because it will not be all happiness and there are many who will not face reality.

In the meantime I exert myself to make up for many years spent and wasted—wasted in that they were unproductive. Like many of my generation I was brought up with the idea that for a girl it was only necessary to know French, take care of one's hands and do one's hair carefully in order to get married and live happily ever after. I did not marry immediately. Contrariness in childhood becomes rebelliousness in girlhood, and the more I realized that marriage was expected of me the more resolutely I prepared my mind for spinsterhood. I remember one summer evening walking home across a square; in a house in which all the curtains were drawn back and the windows opened wide, a ball was going on. One could not hear the music, and the figures revolving silently looked absurd. I seemed to see ourselves as the man in the street sees us.

The impression was indelible. I was bored, too, by my absence of purpose and the unproductiveness of my time.

After that summer evening I spent a good many of my days in Italy. Sometimes in a remote fishing village where I grew to love the people, or in the wilds of Anacapri, beyond the tourist track, and also in Rome and in Florence where the beauty of things enveloped me,—when it was not the little naked bathing figures it was the sculpture I loved; and when the guardian of the museum had turned his back, I would run my fingers over a marble torso, so that my fingertips tingled with emotion and my heart beat faster quite unexplainably.

Sometimes, in contrast to my Italian days, I would spend a winter in Stockholm with the Crown Princess Margaret and the Crown Prince of Sweden. Princess Margaret, who was English (a daughter of the Duke of Connaught), was extremely artistic and painted so well that the leading artists in Sweden declared that if she had not been born a Royalty she would have been a great painter. As it was her duties were too varied to permit of any serious study, but we used to spend whole weeks on painting expeditions and get very absorbed and enthusiastic.

Some of the most interesting artists in Sweden who were her friends used to come and help us and criticize and advise. We worked very hard and made great progress. There was something in the snow scenes that suggested shapes and forms, and my joy in painting them was almost more the joy of form than of color. Form was a subconscious god in my heart.

Then one day the inevitable happened; it was in England, and it was on the longest day of the year, a day which seemed that day all too short.

I got engaged to be married. For four years after that I lived in the country, and during those years I forgot everything except the creation of forms that I was intent upon. The two children which are the result—are my best bits of creative work, and work that will live. We had a Tudor farmhouse near Guildford in Surrey, and at a place near by called Compton, Mrs. Watts, the widow of G. F. Watts had a village pottery. It was quite an ambitious industry; they turned out lovely terra cotta garden pots of Italian design and there were local artists engaged on small allegorical figures. Such an industry in Italy would have been productive of great talent, even of genius, and even in Surrey the effort was not unfruitful.

I used to carry home loads of clay with me, and work out little things of my own. These used to be criticized and approved by Mrs. Watts, and so I began in a humble dilettante way.

When the little flickering flame within me began to develop into a burning fire of ambition; when it dawned on me that dead clay could be brought to life,—a husband who was rather clairvoyant, and doubtless had visions of a neglected home, said "no"—and the flame was suppressed into a rather sullen domesticity.

What next? The war, unexpected and overwhelming!

The abandoned home, the pursuit of arms, the collapse of a business firm, a shattered outlook.

Then the birth of a son, and six days later widowhood. I rose from my childbed and viewed the same scene, but knew it was another world. It has been another world ever since. The smoldering flame rekindled, was fed and heaped with fuel.—A great friend of mine, John Tweed, a former pupil of Rodin, asked me to go to work in his studio. There I met Professor Lanteri, who offered to teach me in his own private studio at the South Kensington College of Art. Princess Patricia, who was a friend of my girlhood, offered, for fun, to sit for me. Professor Lanteri helped me to achieve of her a statuette which I exhibited creditably. Shortly afterwards the Professor died. He was one of the saints of this world, he even had the face of a saint. I missed him terribly; he had been a wonderful friend. His death forced me to stand on my own feet and in a new world. But that world began to give me orders for portraits, so I ran before I could walk; I learnt to walk (and to crawl too) afterwards!

For five years I studied as I earned, and I crammed all the work that my pent up forces made me do. I had luck, and I had love of the work and 'great health. Belief, imagination and capacity for work will carry one a long way on the roughest of roads. Mine, I know, is still a long road to travel, and I like, too, to feel that the end of it is still very far away. I have tried to describe the road that I have traveled up to the present point, and perhaps it will explain?

Meanwhile, the diary opens on the day when I met Kamenev in London. It seems an abrupt beginning, but whatever went before had very little connection. It is often through little accidents that one's life is altered. I had been engaged to go yachting with some friends in August I had worked very hard for a year and was badly in need of a holiday. The yacht at the last moment ran ashore and had to go into dock. The day I should have gone yachting was the day my friend asked me if I would like to meet Kamenev and Krassin.

I jumped at it, having a great curiosity to meet a Bolshevik, for I felt mystified and completely ignorant about them. I had often thought that if I could choose out of the whole world a head to portray, I would select Lenin as the most interesting, illusive and unattainable! I never dreamt that the chance would come.

I have been asked why I, a woman alone, ventured into the Bolshevik midst? I claim that the mere fact of being a woman alone arouses the chivalry of those one meets. Every one's protection is better than some one's. I felt in Moscow what I have felt since I landed in New York, the instinctive chivalry of man towards a stranger in his midst.

But here I must end, for my book has already gone to print, and a messenger is standing at the door waiting to snatch this foreword. He reminds me of how G. F. Watts pursued his colossal figure of "Physical Energy" and continued to work on it as it was being carried away to the bronze foundry. Watts was not a sculptor but his "Physical Energy" expressed what was in Watts. I am not a writer and spiritually I pursue this on its way to print, even as Watts; and as desperately, and too late see the things that want putting right.

CLARE SHERIDAN.

NEW YORK, Feb. 12, 1921

MOSCOW

AUGUST 14TH, 1920. Saturday.

According to Mr. Fisher's instructions, I called on Mr. M—at his office at 10:30 and introduced myself.

He took me in a taxi to Bond 'Street to the office of Messrs. Kamenev and Krassin. We waited for about twenty minutes in an ante-chambre, and I felt a certain melodramatic thrill.

Here was I, at all events in the outer den of these wild beasts who have been represented as ready to spring upon us and devour us! This movement that has caused consternation to the world, and these people, so utterly removed from my environment, these myths of what seemed almost a great legend, I was now quite close to. Meanwhile, the clerks in the office occupied my attention. They interested me as types, and I wondered about them, about exactly WHAT in their lives 'had made them into Bolsheviks, and what sort of mentality was theirs and whether the schemes they upheld were developing into a workable concern.

While we waited Mr. M put me straight on a few points and pointed out many of the inaccuracies about Bolshevism that people like myself have gleaned, so I was in part prepared and protected against appearing too, ignorant and foolish.

At last the word came and we were ushered into the office of Mr. Kamenev who received me amiably and smilingly. We started off almost immediately, in French, and discussed the subject of his being willing to sit to me. I then asked him if a Soviet Government had obliterated Art in Russia. He looked at me for a moment in astonishment, and then said: "Mais non! Artists are the most privileged class."

I asked if they were able to, earn a living wage.

He replied that they were paid higher than the Government Ministers. He gave me fully to understand that Russia is most appreciative of Art and Talent and is anxious to surround itself with culture. He thought the bust had better be started soon, as one never knew what might happen from one moment to the next, "what caprice of Monsieur Lloyd George" might elect to send him out of the country at a moment's notice. So we decided on Tuesday next, at 10 A.M. Mr.Kamenev then took us downstairs to Krassin's office. Mr. Krassin seemed very busy and preoccupied, had some one in the room and didn't quite know what I had come about, but he agreed to sit to me Wednesday next at 10 A. M.

AUGUST 17TH, 1920. Tuesday.

Kamenev arrived nearly punctually at 10 A. M. for an hour, but he stayed till 1 o'clock, and we talked the whole three hours, almost without stopping. I don't know how I managed to work and talk so much. My mind was really more focused on the discussion, and the work was done subconsciously. At all events when the three hours were ended, I had produced a likeness.

There is very little modeling in his face; it is a perfect oval, and his nose is straight with the line of his forehead, but slightly turns up at the end, which is a pity. It is difficult to make him look serious, as he smiles all the time. Even when his mouth is severe his eyes laugh.

My "Victory" was unveiled when he arrived, and he noticed it at once. I told him it represented the Victory of the Allies, and he exclaimed: "But, no! It is the Victory of all the ages.... What pain! What suffering! What exhaustion!..." He then added that it was the best bit of peace propaganda he'd seen.

We had a wonderful conversation. He told me all kinds of details of the Soviet legislation, their ideals and aims. Their first care, he told me, is for the children; they are the future citizens and require every protection. If parents are too poor to bring up their children, the State will clothe, feed, harbor and educate them until fourteen years old, legitimate and illegitimate alike, and they do not need to be lost to their parents, who can see them whenever they wish. This system, he said, had doubled the percentage of marriages (civil of course) it had also allayed a good deal of crime—for what crimes are not committed to destroy illegitimate children?

He described the enforced education of all classes—he told of the concerts they organize for their workmen, and of their appreciation of Bach and Wagner.

They have had to abandon (already!) the idea that all should be paid alike. Admitting that some are physically able to work longer and better than others, he granted therefore that there have to be grades of payment, and that when great talent shows itself, "cela merite d'etre recompense."

Chaliapin, who used to have the title of "Artist to the Court," is now called "The Artist of the People." Chaliapin, I gathered, was a very popular figure.

After awhile Kamenev let drop a suggestion which did not fall on barren ground—he threw it out apparently casually, but I believe to see how I reacted to it. I had just been telling him that I had all my life a love of Russian literature, Russian music, Russian dancing, Russian art, and he said, "You should come to Russia."

I said I had always dreamed it—and that perhaps—who knows—some day....

He said: "You can come with me and I will get you sittings from Lenin and Trotsky."

I thought he was joking, and hesitated a moment, then I said: "Let me know when you are going to start and I will be ready in half an hour."

He offered to telegraph immediately to Moscow for permission!

AUGUST 18TH, 1920. Wednesday.

Krassin arrived at 10 A. M. and found me reading the papers, sitting on the seat outside the door. Like Kamenev he stayed until r o'clock.

He has a beautiful head and he sat almost sphinxlike, severe and expressionless most of the time.

We talked, of course, but his French is less good than Kamenev's, and we broke into occasional German—it was a bad mix-up, but we said all we wanted to say!

Kamenev had talked to him about me and told him of the project of my going to Moscow. I said nothing about it till he first broached it. What impresses me about these two men is their impassive imperturbability, their calm, and their patience. I suppose it is the race, or else they learnt calm when they were prisoners in Siberia.

They are such a contrast to almost all other sitters, who are restless, hurried and fidgety. Krassin is sphinx-like. He sits erect, his head up, and his pointed, bearded chin sticking defiantly out at an angle, and his mouth tightly shut. He has no smile like Kamenev and his piercing eyes just looked at me impassively while I worked. It's rather uncanny.

Krassin is a Siberian. He explained to me that his father was a Government local official and that his mother was a peasant and one of twenty-two children. He himself was the eldest of seven and was brought up in Siberia.

At 1 o'clock I thanked him profusely for sitting so long and so well, and he seemed quite surprised at my stopping, and said: "You have done with me?"

I explained that I had to catch a train, so, having swallowed a fish and some plums, I rushed down the alley to my taxi, pursued by Rigamonte, who abandoned his marble chisel and carried my suitcase and hurled in some last things to me.

I just caught the I:so at Waterloo, to Godalming, to stay two days with the Middletons.

AUGUST 21st, 1920. Saturday.

I got back to the studio about midday to find a huge bunch of roses and the following note from Kamenev:

London, 21st Aout.

Chere Madame, Je vous prie la permission de mettre ces roses rouges aux pieds de votre belle statue de la Fictoire. Bien a vous, L. K

[Dear Madam, I beg your permission to put these red roses at the feet of a beautiful statue of the Fictoire. Bien to you.]

I did so, and when he came at 4 o'clock to sit, I thanked him, but said they weren't red and that it was a pity. He looked as if he didn't understand, and said: "Yes, they are red—red for the blood of Victory." The sentiment was right, but he is color blind, the roses are pink! I didn't argue.

At about 5 o'clock S—L—walked in unexpectedly, and was awfully surprised and interested at finding Kamenev, who was no less interested at hearing from S—L—that Archbishop Mannix is his guest, and I got a good inning at my work while these two talked some pretty plain stuff.

Kamenev and I dined later at the Cafe Royal, and then went on to a Revue which was very bad, but the audience laughed a good deal, and Kamenev wondered at their childish appreciation of rubbish.

AUGUST 22nd 1920. Sunday.

Twelve hours with Kamenev 111

He arrived at 11 A. M. with a huge album of photographs of the Revolution—very interesting., After looking at it he sat to me for an hour. We lunched at Claridge's. After lunch we went for a taxi drive along the embankment, and passing the Tate Gallery, went in. It is being rearranged, but we found the Burne-Jones that Kamenev was looking for. He stood for a long time before "The King and the Beggar Maid." I suppose in the new system all the beggar maids are queens, and the real kings sit at their feet.

At 4 o'clock we went to Trafalgar Square to see what was going on. The Council of Action were having a meeting. Kamenev assured me he must not go near the platform, or be recognized by his friends, as he was under promise to the Government to take no part in demonstrations, nor to do any propaganda work. However, I dragged him by the hand to the outskirts of the crowd, and for no reason that I can explain; the shout went up: "Gangway for speakers," and a channel opened up before us and we were rushed along it.

Happily for Kamenev, there was a hitch as we approached the platform. The crowd thought a policeman was favoritizing us, and getting us to the platform, and a youngish man said, "Stop that, policeman, this is a democratic meeting!" and tried to prevent us going any farther. For a while I felt the hostility of the people around me.

One of the speakers, referring to the spirit of 1914, said we had given our husbands and sons then, but we didn't mean ever to give them again, and I, thinking of my boy, Dick, joined in the shouts of "Never, never!" with some feeling, and I felt the atmosphere kindlier around me after that. When Lansbury tried to speak he was acclaimed with cheers and had to wait patiently while they sang: "For he's a jolly good fellow," and cheered him again.

He seemed to me to talk less of "Class" and more of "Cause." Just for a second he paused, saying, "What we have to do, is to stop...."

I filled in the gap with "Mesopotamia." Whereupon the crowd shouted: "Hear! hear!" and "God bless you!" After that I was one of them.

Then some one recognized Kamenev and the whisper went round and spread like wildfire. The men on either side of him asked if they might announce he was there, to which he answered a most emphatic "No."

When Lansbury had finished speaking there was an appeal for money for the "Cause." It was interesting to watch the steady rain of coins, and very touching to see how the poor gave their pennies. Lansbury buried his face in his hat to shield himself from the metallic rain.

After that we went away, and a gangway was made for us, and all along the whisper went of "Kamenev," and the faces that looked at us were radiant as though they beheld a saviour.

We took a taxi and drove to Hampton Court, and there went outside the garden and into the park to get away from the Sunday crowd. We sat on his coat on the grass in the middle of an open space, and the air was heavy and the sun fitful, as though a storm impended. The distant elms were heavy green. There was a great stillness and calm.

We talked about the meeting, and of the magnetism of a crowd. He noticed my suppressed excitement, for I had blood to the head.

If we had been rushed to the platform I could have spoken to the people, I'm sure I could. He said he had been terribly moved to speak, and it had been a great effort to hold back.

We talked and talked, and then some raindrops forced us to get up and return to the Mitre Hotel for dinner. After dinner the weather cleared and we had a lovely hour and a half in a boat on the river. There was a three-quarter moon, and the water reflected the pink lights from the Chinese lanterns of the houseboats. From the garden of Hampton Court rose up what seemed to be a giant cypress tree silhouetted against the dusk, and the reflection of it doubled its height. It was like something in Italy. I rowed the boat, which I loved doing, and Kamenev hummed Volga boatman songs. Or else we broke back into discussions, and then he forgot he was steering and we had several slight collisions and narrow escapes from more serious ones I

It was a very successful evening, and we came back by the last train to Waterloo, still talking, chiefly about that impending and all absorbing visit to Moscow, and we parted on my doorstep at a quarter to midnight.

AUGUST 24TH, 1920. Tuesday.

I felt ill, but got up early, expecting Krassin at 10, but at 1:00 I got a telephoné message to the effect that neither Mr. Krassin nor Mr. Kamenev could see me to-day as the political crisis had caused a deluge of work.

Lloyd George at Lucerne had taken exception to the clause in the Russian Peace Terms, demanding that the Polish Civic Militia should be drawn from the working classes. This they say is an infringement of the liberty of Poland. Truth to tell, it's the Polish success over the Red Army that has caused this diplomatic volte face. However, this is too big a subject to go into here.

At dinner time Kamenev telephoned me it was his first breathing space, and could he come and see me. I asked him to take pot-luck for dinner, and he arrived, a battered and worn fighting man.

Full of indignation, but still full of fight and hope and belief.

He stayed till 11, and said he felt better. It was very still here, and the peace did him good.

There may be a "state of war" in a few days, and as things now stand they all depart on Friday. Great excitement, as I shall go with them.

AUGUST 25TH, 1920. Wednesday.

Krassin gave me my second sitting at 5 P. M. and stayed till 7:30. I heard all the latest news.

He's a delightful man, and I've never done a head I admired more. He seems to be strong morally, to a degree of adamant. He is calm, sincere, dignified, proud, with self-consciousness and without vanity. Scientific in his analysis of things and people. Eyes that are unflinching and bewilderingly direct, nostrils that dilate with sensitiveness, a mouth that looks hard until it smiles, and a chin full of determination.

AUGUST 26TH, 1920. Thursday.

Krassin offered me a third sitting and came again at 5 and stayed till after 7. War is averted, and he assures me that Kamenev under no excuse can possibly leave for Russia before a fortnight. I did not sleep much, waking up with the exclamation, "Partons! Partons!" for if we don't get away before a fortnight I shall have to keep my engagement to go on September 1oth to Oxford to the Birkenheads to do F. E. and then I shall not get to Russia before my exhibition.

I worked hard, and Krassin's head is finished.

I think it's good. Sidney came to see me after dinner, and we talked fantastically about Russia, and what it might or might not lead to! He is terribly interested.

AUGUST 27TH, 1920. Friday.

Kamenev came at eleven to give me a last sitting. He was in a much happier frame of mind, chuckling over Tchitcherin's reply to Lloyd George, which is an impudent bit of propaganda work, and ALL the papers HAVE to publish it because it is official!

I waked up this morning with an excited and tired feeling, my hands trembling, which I've never known before. Kamenev arrived in much the same condition. He talked politics, and got excited and worked up and produced the quizzical frown that I wanted. I worked well, and absolutely changed the whole personality of his bust, which I think he liked.

He promised incidentally not to wait here two weeks, but says he will start NOT LATER than next Friday. I wonder if he keeps 'his promises.

Peter turned up with a girl, which, disturbed the sitting and I felt more and more hectic, what with the difficulties and the battle of it, and knowing that it was the last sitting, and feeling dead beat, and having finally to stop for lunch.

Kamenev and I lunched with Sidney Cooke at Claridge's. I introduced them to each other, and we are going to stay with Sidney at his house in the Isle of Wight, for the week-end. Like all good foreigners Kamenev expressed a desire, some days ago, to see the Isle of Wight. So it is arranged. I had meant to go to my beloved Dick, but I sent him a crocodile by Peter, to compensate.

Dined with Aunt Jennie; she has laryngitis, and looked very ill. We dined in the drawing-room. She asked me what new work I was engaged on, but I took good care not to mention Russians nor Russia.

In the course of conversation she told me I was being criticized as having too much freedom. I chuckled over this as I visualized to myself the great band of people who grudge me that freedom, because they have not got it, and because they know that freedom counts above everything.

I said to Aunt Jennie, "And how is that grave condition of things, that dangerous 'Liberty' going to be rectified? I am a widow and earning my living, how is it to be otherwise ordered?"

She had no suggestion. It would have been obviously out of place to suggest re-marriage, which in fact is the only way of ending everything, liberty, work, my happiness, which is dependent on my work.

AUGUST 28TH, 1920. Saturday.

I left the studio in a state of chaos, Smith being in the midst of casting Kamenev and Krassin. I felt a wonderful sensation of relief, at these being finished, and the Victory also. Everything for the moment is finished, until I begin something new. And who will that be I wonder?

Kamenev picked me up at 12: I S and we caught a 12.50 from Waterloo to Portsmouth. Sidney* met us at the Harbor, and escorted us to his house on the Isle of Wight, near Newport. A very attractive journey across, as it was warm and calm weather. A motor met us at Ryde and took us to his house, seven miles. On arrival we flung ourselves down in the sun on the grass of the tennis-court. And after tea, as we lay full length on rugs, our heads leaning on the grassy bank behind us, and the sun gradually sinking lower and lower, Kamenev for over an hour told us the history of the Russian Revolution.

He told it to us haltingly, stumbling along in his bad French, wrestling with words and phrases, but always conveying his meaning and, above all, conjuring up the most graphic pictures,— making us see with his eyes, live over the days with him, and know all the people concerned. He is amazingly forceful and eloquent.

We sat silent and spell-bound. He began as far back as twenty years ago, with the first efforts of himself and Lenin, Trotsky and Krassin. He described their secret organizations, their discoveries, their arrests, his months and years of prison, first in cells, then in Siberia—but long before he had finished, our dinner was proclaimed, and we went in just as we were to eat. The spell for the moment was broken, and though he did not again that evening

18

resume the tale of the Revolution, he did most of the evening's talking.

He described to us shortly but vividly the individuality and psychology of Lenin. There were others also, the president of the extraordinary Commission, a man turned to stone through years of "traveaux force," an ascetic and a fanatic, whom the Soviet selected as organizer and head of "La Terreur."

This is the man of whom Maxim Gorky wrote "that one could see martyrdom crystallized in his eyes." He performs his arduous task, suffering over it, but with the conviction that he is helping towards an ultimate reign of peace and calm, towards which end every means is justified. This man sleeps in a narrow bed behind a curtain in his "bureau" and has few friends, and cares for no women, but he is kind to children, and considerate towards his fellow-workers when they are overworked or ill.

It is useless to try to tell any of Kamenev's stories, they require his individuality, and would lose in repeating. I only felt that it was a great waste that his audience consisted only of us two, when so many might have been enthralled.

AUGUST 29TH, 1920. Sunday.

When I came down from breakfast I found the two men sitting over a fire. I accused them of "frousting," and carried them out to the garden, and Kamenev restarted his unconcluded tale of the Revolution, until we could bear the cold no more, so he finished indoors in front of the fire.

It is a marvelous narrative, pray God, I may never forget it.

At 2:30, the afternoon having mended, we started off in an open car for the south of the Island. On a hill overlooking the sea, with a lonely beach, we stopped, and made a long arduous descent. It was heavenly on the undulating beach of tiny rounded pebbles, by the sea edge.

Sidney and I paddled and Kamenev, who watched us, became thoroughly laughing and happy. When Sidney and I sat down on the beach and buried our feet in the pebbles, Kamenev began to write verses to me on the back of a five pound note.

I don't know what happened to the bank note, but Kamenev wrote four lines, and Sidney the other four, in French. Kamenev likened me to Venus, but Sidney was flippant, and said that the part of me he liked best was my feet!

The scenery and climb recalled Capri, but a faded Capri without color. Nevertheless, one re membered the feeling of joy one had at Capri, and Kamenev was much impressed by the beauty and the peace of it, and said how distant politics seemed, and how non-existent Mr. Lloyd George!

[*David Lloyd George, 1st Earl Lloyd-George of Dwyfor, O.M. P.C. (1863–1945); British Liberal politician and statesman.*]

After awhile, we regretfully went on, stopping only for a tea-picnic on a common off a lonely road.

SEPTEMBER 2ND, 1920. Thursday.

Brede Place.

I have been here since Monday. Papa is away in Ireland fishing, Mamma is here and believes I am still going yachting and that a telegram will call me away at any minute. As no wire has come, and I cannot bear the suspense, I've decided to go up to London, for the day, and shall go straight to Kamenev's office from the station. So I'll know soon whether we start for Russia on Saturday or not. If we do I shall not come back here.

I wonder what it will be. To-night, when I said good-night to Dick he clung to me more than usual, and we talked together for a long time.

He held me tight. I was kneeling on the ground next his 'bed, with my arms round him. He said he could not bear to let me go. He said he would tie me up to a wall and cover me with kisses, and not let me go to-morrow. He was terribly sweet, and I felt a great reluctance at leaving him.

Should anything happen to me if I go on this expedition I want Peter (Oswald, my brother), to take great care of Dick. I don't know what money there would be to help him, but some of my widow's pension would be paid to the children from the Government.

I would like Aunt Leonie, whom I love dearly, and whose judgment I value, to lend Peter a hand, for Mamma is not strong enough to take it on.

Also, darling though she is, we are so opposite in our views of life and the future.

I want Dick to be very modern, very Liberal.

I want him to have a chance of being fully whatever he thinks is right, even if it does not agree with those who surround him. So long as he is sincere, and convinced he is right, then he is right.

St. John and Madeleine Middleton will, I know, ask him to Peper Harrow. The Sheridan family are not likely to start interesting themselves in Dick, as they have not done so up to the present.

The Wavertrees, however, have begun to love Margaret, and are looking after her and she is happy. I suppose if anything happens to me she will be permanently with them. I am grateful to Sophie and thankful. I think all is well with Margaret, and her problem is far more easily settled than Dick's.

But I do wish she could be brought up to be purposeful, not luxurious, and to feel that she will have a career. Work alone brings happiness, and the desire to achieve or to attain is the only satisfaction.

However, if I am no more, they may be brought up very differently from my plans, but they will undoubtedly develop into something because they have individuality. But it is all in the hands of the gods.

To Peter I leave the remains of my seven years' lease of the studio. My jewels to Margaret, except a ruby and diamond ring which is already Peter's. My books to Dick, also my diaries and letters.

I have not much to leave, my philosophy of life is to travel light and not accumulate, but to throw off.

I think the money I have in the bank and the money I am owed should pay my debts.

I don't care what happens to my work. I've worked hard and done my best. I hoped to make a name for myself. I am ambitious to do good work. It's a very, very long road to climb, and I'd like to get further along it—but this is a great adventure and worth doing—and I'm rather tired of the great uncertainty of the future, and so, if it all ends so soon it ends well. I've had four years of glorious happy work, and I leave two beautiful children to be my immortality.

To these I say: "Work, Work, always Work."

Don't turn your backs on the World's new doctrines, not even if you have something to lose. If you have something to lose, lose it in the cause.

Fight for the cause, if you believe it to be right.

Remember the millions whose lives are not worth living and who must be helped.

Children, I love you—God bless you.

May this stand as a sort of will in case anything happens to me.

Written at Brede Place, August 23rd, 1920.

SEPTEMBER 3RD, 1920. Friday.

I went up to London and drove straight to the Bolshevik office in Bond Street, and left my luggage waiting outside in the taxi. Unlike the previous occasion, I was not shown straight in to Kamenev. I sat down and waited in the outer room which was full of men, six or seven of them, and they began discussing me in Italian, French, German, and Russian! I tried to look dignified and aloof, and I'm sure I was a great failure as a Bolshevik. All my English conventional breeding took hold of me! Later Peter came to fetch me, thinking I had finished my interview, and then I felt better, having him to talk to. Later an eighth man appeared with a lot of papers and the garrulous crowd became of a sudden serious, and sat round a table, and there seemed to be a sort of council going on.

At this moment Klyschko passed by the open door, and espying me called me and Peter into him room to wait. I asked him why there were so many people in the other room, and he shrugged his shoulders.

At last I was told both Mr. Kamenev and Mr.

Krassin wanted to see me, and I was shown into Krassin's office. I learnt in a moment what I had feared, that our journey is not for to-morrow.

Moscow has answered his application too late.

There was just a faint chance left, for a telegram from Moscow was being deciphered at that moment, but it was almost too slight to count upon.

Krassin asked if he might bring his wife and daughters to the studio at 4 o'clock, and then Kamenev took me up to his office. He held out real hopes of starting next week. There is just a good chance.

As soon as Krassin and his very attractive family, but slightly alarming wife, had left I went to see—, whom I thought was in a position to get the vise I want, for Reval. My passport is all in order to Stockholm but Klyschko has failed to get the Esthonian vise because it is necessary to get the Foreign Office approval to do so.

After three-quarters of an hour's talk with—, I realized that it was hopeless. He merely shared the general prejudice. It confirms me in my decision not to take any one else into my confidence, besides Sidney and S—L—.

They are the only two who have got the spirit to understand.

But how I want that Esthonian vise it is worth an effort to get it, instead of starting with an uncertainty.—explained to me at length, and kindly, why he did not want me to go. He said that he believed a complete change of Government policy was impending, which would make my position in Russia untenable. Moreover, that I would be in great danger of being shot as a spy. He told me what he thought of Lenin and Trotsky (it seemed very much what other people think).

He said that Kamenev was no better than the rest, and that a Russian was capable of turning even upon a friend. Finally he asked me why I wanted to go. I claimed an artist's zeal in wishing to do Lenin and bring his head back in my arms!

He then wanted to know why "they" wanted to take me, to which I could give no clear answer, having wondered somewhat myself. He then tried to draw me on the subject of Bolshevism and asked me: "What do you gather is the final and ultimate object of the Bolsheviks?"

It was a difficult question. I thought for a moment and then I said: "They are very great idealists, it may be an unpractical and unworkable idealism, but that does not alter it."

He was unsurprised at this, and said in a low voice, almost more to himself than to me: "Are they as clever as that—" by which I suppose he meant, had they really been so clever as to take me in!!!

At the end of it all I said to him: "You see in the papers that H. G. Wells is going to Russia?"

He said that Wells could look after himself.

[*Herbert George Wells, author of* War of the Worlds, The Invisible Man, *etc.*]

I claimed to be equally fit to do so, to which he replied: "So you still want to go?"

I explained that I was prepared for anything.

He seemed surprised but practically consented to try and get my passport put in order for me, and asked me to go and see him again next week.

I got back in time to dine with Kamenev at "Canuto's." After dinner, it being a lovely warm evening, we took an open taxi and I suggested driving to Hampstead Heath. Arrived there, we left the taxi on the main road, while we went on foot off a side road on to a rough sandy track, quite away from people and lights.

On a bank I spread my white fur coat and we sat there for an hour or more. It was very beautiful. The tall pine stems stood out against the glowing sky of distant, flaring London. The place was full of depth and distance and night mystery. I talked to Kamenev about my conversation with a friend, who was a serious intelligent man, and told him of his opinion that I should be in danger of my life. I added I was prepared to take the risk, but that I should regret my children being orphans. Kamenev answered me half amused, half irritated.

He said it was such nonsense that he fell a great desire to start immediately so as to show me the truth, and so that I might come back and prove to all and sundry how ignorant they are of real conditions.

He considered that no matter what line the Government adopted here (and he was prepared that Lloyd George might do anything at any moment), it would not be vented upon me. I should be regarded purely as an artist and international non-political.

Then laughing, he said he would have me put against a wall, arms crossed on breast (not blindfolded, that was a convention of the aristocrats!) , and a firing party should take aim, and he would save me at the last moment. Just so that I might live through every thrill, and my friends be disappointed!

He told me incidentally that Wrangel is defeated and discredited (... having just told me that Wrangel had won the peasants over to him, and that he had a scheme of moderate Government, and was likely to rouse a counter-revolution and depose the present lot).

So I said to Kamenev: "Where is truth?"

And he answered: "There is no truth in the world, the only truth is in one's heart."

SEPTEMBER 9TH, 1920. Thursday.

My birthday, and the most hectic of my life!

In the morning I worked more or less calmly, The "Victory" was just being finished, Smith was chipping away the last remains of mold. Rigamonte, under my direction, was punching the blocks of Princess Pat, so that marble chips flew like shrapnel in all directions.

Meanwhile Hart came to get my last orders about marble pedestals for unfinished bronzes, and on top of all Fiorini turned up.

He was terribly hurt because I have given the heads of Kamenev and Krassin to Parlanti to cast.

He had dreamed of doing them—he had a Bolshevik workman in his foundry, who asked every day when those heads were coming. He would have cast them, he said, for nothing, just for the honor and glory of doing them.... I felt terribly badly about it. The little Italian man is such an enthusiast, and he met Kamenev here, who shook hands with him, and Fiorini felt about it as most people about their King. On that occasion he hid behind a pedestal, and remained so quiet for a quarter of an hour, watching me and my sitter, that I forgot he was there.

But because I understood from Fiorini that he had as much work as he could get through for me in time for my exhibition, I had given the heads to Parlanti, who promised them in time.

I hope I comforted him by promising to give him the duplicates to cast, as presents to Kamenev and Krassin, the which I had had no intention of doing, and can ill afford, but to cheer up Fiorini I will do it.

Then the telephone went and Klyschko announced to me that it was all decided—Kamenev is starting on Saturday morning, has reserved places and I have nothing to do but get my ticket.

I said I was having difficulties over my passport, and he explained to me that all I need get is the vise via Christiania to Stockholm, and that at Stockholm the Esthonian Legation would see me through.

I dined with Sophie Wavertree and F. M. B.

Fisher. He walked me home. He it is who originally brought me in touch with this wonderful new world.

SEPTEMBER 10TH 1920. Friday.

Kamenev telephoned at breakfast. He is really starting to-morrow.

At 10:15 a wire from Sidney, to say he's arriving from Scotland at 5:00.

11:30 to Barclay's Bank, cashed £100.

11:40 to Cook's, bought my ticket.

12:00 Bond Street Office, saw Kamenev. He says it doesn't matter about a passport, that he can push me through from Stockholm o'clock, bought a hat in South Molton Street.

2 o'clock, back at studio. Wrote letters all afternoon.

4:30 hair washed and cut.

7:00 back to studio, packed and dined.

10:30 Sidney came, and while we were talking Kamenev rang up to say he had had a few short hours ago an interview with Lloyd George, and that he gathered from the interview that he, Kamenev, leaves to-morrow, not to return—this was pour me prevenir [to prevent me]—but he said, come all the same.

I rang up S L, who could hardly believe that I am really starting. He came round to see me and we three talked far into the night.

SEPTEMBER 11TH, 1920. Saturday.

Mr. Krassin, and most of the 128 New Bond Street staff were at St. Pancras to see us start.

Krassin presented me with a big box of chocolates tied up with red ribbons. We were rather a conspicuous group on the platform. I feared every second to meet some one I knew traveling, possibly to York, on the same train.

L— was there to wish me God-speed, and Sidney, who is staying with friends near Newcastle and came down yesterday to spend my last evening with me, traveled back to Newcastle with us. Rigamonte turned up unexpectedly, which touched me very much.

Sidney, fulfilling his reputation as an organizer, discovered there were two trains going to Newcastle, and that the next one starting a little later had a restaurant car, so we transferred our luggage from the one to the other, and in the process I lost my handbag which had my hundred pounds in it in bank notes, all I possessed in the world!

It caused me some agitation, but Kamenev was quite calm and seemed to think that money was not very important, and that I should not have much need of it in Russia.

To my intense relief, however, Sidney found the case at Newcastle in the lost property office.

It traveled ahead of us on the other train.

Sidney came to the ship with us. I don't think he believed in the reality of my journey until he saw me safely past the passport officials!

I certainly felt no sense of security until the steamer left the quay-side. There was something indescribably exciting and clandestine about slipping away without any one knowing.

For some time Kamenev and I stood on deck to see the last of England, with her Turner sky.

The sunset was golden haze, and Kamenev said:

"It looks mysterious, that land, doesn't it?" But to me it was just the old world wrapt in a shroud.

Mystery lay ahead of us in the new world that is our destination.

Now for the first time I have leisure and calm in which to think over what I am doing. There persist in my mind faint echoes of warnings, but I must have no misgivings. It seems to me unlikely that Kamenev would invite me to go to his country if I were likely to be either unhappy or in danger there. There are moments in life when it is necessary to have blind faith.

SEPTEMBER 1 2TH, Sunday. In my cabin on board S. S. Jupiter.

It is 9:45 P. M. We have just this moment come alongside the quay-side at Bergen. We are not to land till to-morrow morning. The crossing has been wonderful, as calm as a lake the whole way.

I have a cabin for three all to myself; there are very few people on board. It is comfortable as a yacht. The only fellow traveler we have spoken with is an American calling himself Comrad Costello. He reports for the Federated Press (new service for the Socialist Press).

A perfectly keen journalist, typically American, and not letting the grass grow under his feet.

For an hour this afternoon I did interpreter between him and Kamenev. I had to ask about strange people and strange things that I knew nothing about. I had not even heard of Debs before.

I expect I shall have a pretty good knowledge of all the Revolutionary Leaders in all countries before long.

Kamenev had a cigarette in my cabin this evening, and we discussed Philosophy, Religion, and Revolution. It surprised me very much that he does not believe in God. He says that the idea of God is a domination and that he resents it, as he resents all other dominations. He talked nevertheless with great admiration of the teachings of Christ, who demanded poverty and equality among men, and who said that the rich man had no more chance of the Kingdom of Heaven than a camel of getting through a needle's eye.

SEPTEMBER 13TH, Grand Hotel, Christiania.

Monday.

To-day might have been many days, and we might have been crossing the world.

The train left Bergen at 8:15 A. M. We had a compartment to ourselves with big windows.

Slowly from Voss the train climbed higher and higher. The higher we went the less vegetation there was. Big trees became smaller trees, and then dwarf trees and then shrub, until finally there was only the little low creeper juniper.

There were rocks and boulders, falling torrents and cold still lakes, and in, the shadow of the mountains great patches of snow that never melt.

This morning in the breakfast car we eagerly asked for news, being unable to read Norwegian.

The man who was reading the paper informed us in broken English that the coal strike was exactly the same, and the Lord

Mayor of Cork not dead yet. With that summary we had to rest content.

Later in the morning the dining-car attendant sought us out, and armed with a newspaper said:

"Have you heard the news?" He then made a bow and asked: "Mr. Kamenev yes?" and showed him a photograph of Kamenev in the morning's paper, and the information that he had left England and was on his way to Russia. That settled it. Kamenev was recognized and the car attendant spread the information. After that whenever we walked the platform of a station we were the cynosure of all eyes.

At luncheon Kamenev asked the car attendant, who spoke Russian so well, where he had learnt it. The answer was that fifteen years ago he had spent two years as a waiter in Petrograd. Kamenev told him that Russia was a good deal changed since then and that he ought to go and see it.

The attendant with a deferential smile said he would be afraid to!

At Finse, the highest point, where we were on a level with the mountain summits, and snow lay around us and below us, the train stopped ten minutes. We got out and walked about, I took my kodak. Beyond the platform on the sloping bank, a granite monolith stood up grimly against the snow-patched distance, and to my surprise, engraved upon it were the names of Captain Scott and all his party, with the date, and the announcement that they had started from Norway for the South Pole. It was rather emotional finding it so unexpectedly and remote.

At 10 P: M. we steamed into Christiania, where we were met by [Maxim Maximovich] Litvinoff. I had visualized a small sharp-faced, alert man. Instead I found a big, square, amiable, smiling man. He informed us that there was not a room to be had at the Grand Hotel, and turning to me added in English: "If you want rooms in the Grand Hotel you will have to secure them through the British Legation." We all laughed, and I said: "We are not making much use of the British Legation on this trip."

As we entered the Grand Hotel and stepped into the lift I caught the sound of string band music which characterizes the Grand Hotels and Ritz-Carltons of Europe, and suggests all that side of life that we on this trip are not quite in harmony with. Litvinoff accommodated me in the room of one of his secretaries. I felt rather strange, lonely and lost, especially when questioned by one of them as to my work and plans.

Had I been working in the Soviet office in London? I felt rather at a disadvantage, having to explain that I was merely an artist who had done portraits of Kamenev and Krassin (whom, by the way, they spoke of as Comrad), and that I hoped to get through to Russia, with Kamenev, to do some portraits there.

I felt, as they looked at me, that I did not look much like a sculptor. They proceeded to tell me that no British passports were being issued, and that any amount of people were being held up here. Very cheerful! By this time I had drunk three cups of excellent tea out of a tumbler, and it was nearly midnight and I suggested bed, apologizing at the same time for making use of their room and necessitating their discomfort.

It being now 1 o'clock, I propose to sleep, though I am only wrapped in my rug, for the bed is not made up for me and I do not like sleeping in other people's sheets! The noise in the street is perfectly infernal and Kamenev and Litvinoff are still talking in the next room on my other side.

SEPTEMBER 14TH, 1920, Christiania, Tuesday.

Slept very well wrapped in my rug. Woke up at 9 and had breakfast in bed. Had terribly looked forward to a bath but the sour-faced hotel maid says there are too many gentlemen who want it, and so I cannot. This does not seem an adequate reason for denying it to me and I rather suspect it is part of a general boycott of Bolsheviks.

While I was breakfasting Kamenev looked in with the morning papers which have come out with headlines and photographs of him. One described him as having arrived "with a lady, tall and elegant, who carried in one hand a 'kodakaparat' and in the other a

31

box of sweets—she does not look Russian, and was heard to speak French."

At luncheon I met Mrs. Litvinoff and was surprised to find that she is English, a friend of the Meynells and of H. G. Wells. She has short black hair and is unconventional. She did not seem to be very political or revolutionary. The third baby is imminent.

After luncheon we made an expedition outside Christiania to the wireless station which is on the top of a wooded hill from which there is a magnificent view. Misha, the eldest child, a boy of four accompanied us. He is unruly, wild-eyed, and most attractive,—the embodiment of Donatello's "laughing boy." He says: "What for is my father a Bolshevist?" and tells his mother to ring the bell for the maid and not to do any work herself.

Litvinoff adores him and throws him about and makes him stand on his head. Coming home, Litvinoff and I, hatless, ran races down the hill. To my great humiliation he outran me. He is a heavy man and I run well, but he was not even out of breath!

On the way back in the open car, they all sang Russian folk songs in a chorus. Bolsheviki are a very cheerful species!

We reached the hotel just in time to pick up our luggage and catch the train for Stockholm.

There were real cordial good-bys all round.

Litvinoff said that if I did not get through from Stockholm I must come back to Christiania and he would send some one with me to take me through Murmansk. But Mrs. Litvinoff said I would get through all right. "Those sorts of people always get what they want," she said, but gave no further comment, and I am wondering what sort of person I am.

The two secretaries gave me messages for friends in Moscow and seemed very envious of any one going back. One of them (with most beautiful chestnut hair) held forth to me on the great difference the Revolution had brought into the position of women. She is an ardent Communist and works ten hours a day with a willing heart and little pay. She added as a last appeal:

"Go—and see for yourself, and then say nice things about us when you get back to England."

SEPTEMBER 15TH, 1920, Stockholm.

Wednesday.

We arrived at 8:30 A. M. and were met at the station by Frederick Strom, head of the left wing, Socialist party of Sweden. It was an interesting contrast to my arrival in former years when the Crown Prince himself used to meet me and take me in a royal car to the Palace. I felt a great sadness as I passed that old Palace, and the windows of Princess Margaret's rooms I knew so well.

The days when I used to stay there seemed very long ago and of another world.

We drove to the Grand Hotel which however proved to be full but we were not at a loss: we drove off to a perfectly charming apartment belonging to the Krassins but which in their absence is inhabited by a Comrad Juon.

We were most courteously received and given a splendid breakfast.

Juon is about six feet and a half high, broad in proportion, with a black beard and a kindly expression. His eyes have exceptionally big pupils that give a curious gleam and keenness to his expression. His brother in Russia is a well known painter.

Conversation between the two was mostly in Russian. I am beginning to cultivate a detached feeling, and I do not expect to understand much during the next few weeks except through my eyes.

While we were breakfasting the Grand Hotel telephoned to place a suite of rooms at our disposal. So we returned there, and the Hotel authorities were most civil.

From that moment there ensued hectic uncalm.

Series of newspaper reporters arrived and had to be given interviews.

Comrads came, and stayed—there seemed to be people revolving perpetually. Some of them understood only German, others struggled in bad English, yet others in French, the whole thing mixed up with Swedish and Russian so that one's head reeled.

Among all these people, one figure stands out more clearly than the rest. This is Rjasonoff, a man about seventy with a Greek profile, a beard that stands out defiantly, and hawk's eyes. He has a dominating personality.

This man has done five years of solitary confinement in a cell for the cause. He was charming to me, and his expression lost some of its battle, and became kindly even when he looked at me.

Another man who stands out in my mind is a Communist poet called Torre Norman, who has translated Rupert Brooke.

Mr. Strom accompanied me to the Esthonian Consulate to get my Reval vise. There were, as I expected, endless difficulties, and nothing settled, and to-morrow the boat leaves at 4 so there is not much time. I feel pretty confident that all will end well! It is not possible that there can be any other ending.

We were a big party lunching in the restaurant and attracted a good deal of attention. After lunch we all went to Skansen and had tea there.

In the evening Kamenev had to go out and keep an appointment, and while he was out I wrestled on the telephone with reporters, trying to ward off interviews until the morrow. At 10

P. M. Kamenev came back and we dined in the sitting room. He was pretty dead beat. Even then a reporter came to the door and asked for an interview, but I insisted he must be put off till the next day, and Kamenev, rather willingly, I think, gave in.

SEPTEMBER r 6TH, 1920, Stockholm.

Thursday.

This morning I telephoned to the Palace, and asked for the Crown Prince. Kamenev asked me if I were right to risk it. He said that I might be very ill received in view of the company I was in, but I explained that he was one of the most Democratic Princes in Europe.

Prince Gustav's surprise was indeed pretty great. He was enormously interested and amused and asked me to lunch, and to come at midday so as to get a good talk first.

Kamenev listened to our conversation with some amusement. He told me afterwards that he liked "the tone." I wonder whether he had expected me to be different.

I asked the Prince, as a favor, that Princess Margaret's maid, Amy, might come out shopping with me, and she came and fetched me, and was a tremendous help, as she knew where to take me, and did all the talking in Swedish.

I left her to collect my parcels, as it was nearly midday, got a taxi and told him to drive to "The Palace." He looked vague, and did not understand. I said: "Palace! Kronprinzen." He nodded assent and drove off in a direction that I knew was not the Palace. We fetched up in a street in front of the Kronprinzen Hotel. It was hopeless to argue—I plunged into the hotel and asked for some one who spoke English, and explained my dilemma, to the intense amusement of the hotel officials, and of the taxi driver when it was explained to him.

Prince Gustav looked very lonely in those big rooms and they were extraordinarily vibrant and reminiscent of her. He made me sit down and tell him all about my plans and my adventure, and fell thoroughly into the spirit of the thing. Said I was quite right, if my exhibition at Agnew's for October was all organized, not to sacrifice the chance of this experience, on that account. He thought the expedition a dangerous one, but sensibly admitted that that was my concern, and no one else's.

He asked me, of course, a lot of questions as to what sort of men Kamenev and Litvinoff were. I couldn't help being perfectly frank, and telling him my sincere impressions.

While I was there Kamenev telephoned to say that the Consulate of Esthonia had given me my vise.

At luncheon, the lady-in-waiting and the A.D.C.'s seemed rather bewildered. It certainly must have appeared fantastic to them, accustomed to the dull routine of Court life, to be entertaining some one who was on the way to Russia with Kamenev to sculp the heads of Lenin and Trotsky.

The Prince was overwhelming in his desire to help my material comforts. He telephoned for biscuits, and two large tins arrived, also cigarettes.

He also wrote out his prospective trip to Athens in hopes that possibly we may meet if I come back that way.

He escorted me to the taxi that awaited me in the courtyard, and wished me luck and God-speed.

I returned to the Grand Hotel and found an alarming crowd of Comrads lunching with Kamenev in his sitting-room and we had to leave aL most immediately to catch our boat for Reval.

SEPTEMBER I7TH, 1920, Friday.

It is evening, we have just put in at Hongo, a Finnish port. No one is allowed off the ship, by order of the Port authorities. Finland is not yet at peace with Russia, and Kamenev would probably be arrested if he put a foot on shore. The last time he walked into a Finnish territory in

1917, not knowing the whites were in possession of the town, he was put in prison for three months, and by a miracle was not shot. So far we have had a pretty good journey, and the little boat has hugged the coast of the Oland Islands. We have had to put into Hongo for the night, because we can only steam by day on account of the floating mines between here and Reval that have not yet been cleared.

I have spent half the day in my cabin sleeping, the other half on deck talking. I have lost all track of days and dates, we seem to have been journeying forever.

There are no pleasure trippers or idle curious on board. Practically every one is bound for Russia, and we look at one another curiously, wondering what each other's mission is. There are Cornrads returning, and there are journalists, traders and bankers. People who hope to get through from Reval, and people who probably will, others who certainly won't get through.

Kamenev is watched by every one, and we have made innumerable acquaintances. Already there is a little group of friends around us, whom one has the feeling of having known a long time. Tomorrow we go on to Reval. It seems to me too wonderful and unbelievable that I am really on this boat of fears and dreams: fears of not getting on board, and dreams of the world it would sail me to.

SEPTEMBER 18TH, 1920, Saturday.

At dawn we left Hongo, but there was such a wind blowing that the ship anchored just at the entrance of the harbor, and for a few hours we swung around. No one complained of delay, no one seemed to be in a hurry. There was no attempt to keep a scheduled time. A calm atmosphere of fatalism, which is probably Russian, seemed to hang over us.

The sun was shining brilliantly when we finally set out to sea, and I was having a most interesting conversation with Mr. Aschberg, a Swedish banker, who did me the compliment of talking political economy to me, of which I understood nothing. He told me interesting things about Bolshevik business transactions with Germany, in which it seemed that the Bolsheviks were alienating the German workers by negotiating with the German capitalists.

In my own mind I did not see how they could do otherwise but my ignorance on these things is so great that I try to learn all I can without giving myself away by asking too many questions.

It is a slow process, but I have hopes. The mere fact of being under the wing of a man like Kamenev, and bound for Russia, seems to make people talk to me as if I were a man. It is a great comfort no longer to meet people on a social or superficial ground. There were people, even who talked to me on most obscure subjects, and asked for my intercession for them with Kamenev!

At sunset we steamed into Reval, where the pointed towers and the sound of old bells, as in Italy, awakened one to a new atmosphere that was no longer Scandinavian. A motor met us at the quay, the only motor there, and a man who had crossed with us, and whom I suspected of being a British agent, said to me ironically as he drove away in a droshki: "How very smart and distinguished of you to have a motorI, Kamenev's boy of 12 met us, and there were two small children as well, belonging to Gukofski, the Soviet representative at Reval. They took up most of the room that was needed for luggage.

Alexandre Kamenev had to stand on the step outside, and a soldier of the Red Army on the other.

Thus our curious car-load made its way, hooting loudly through medieval tortuous streets.

What followed is rather nebulous in my mind.

I was very tired and the town very dark, there were stars overhead, but no street lamps. We drove to some bleak building calling itself the Hotel Petersbourg, which seemed to be the Bolshevik G.H.Q. It was dirty and grim, and full of strange looking people who talked nothing that I understood. They looked at me strangely, a great many hands shook mine. Kamenev was too busy to explain to me what our plans were, or what was going to happen next, or maybe he forgot that I could not understand. He was too surrounded for me to be able to ask him any questions, so I just looked vague, waited about and followed,. relying on my eyes to convey the explanations that my ears were denied! Kamenev was the center of perpetual discussions in which every one spoke at the same moment, very quickly and very loud.

At first I suspected a most agitating State Council, but it turned out to be merely a discussion as to where we should have supper. Finally it was decided that we should go to the apartment in a hotel where the wife of a Comrad would look after us. Off we went on foot over cobblestones.

The streets were full of people who moved like shadows, and one could only see faces when they passed the glare of a lighted doorway.

We followed along in couples. At my side was Alexandre Kamenev, a nice boy and friendly, but he could talk only Russian.

We got to the hotel (such a hotel! more like a wayside inn). We were taken to the Comrad's apartment, where his wife received us with great cordiality and talked to me in good French.

There was a samovar, and we had excellent tea with lemon in it, and some cold smoked salmon on thick pieces of buttered bread. Kamenev and two Comrads were too absorbed in their discussion to eat anything. One Comrad was telling something; Kamenev took notes, and our host, a small nervous man, rolled bread pellets.

Madame in an even tenor plied me with questions:

"When did you leave London?"

"How long did you take from Stockholm to, Reval? Oh dear—a day and a half late! We have no news here, tell me some."

"Is Comrad Kamenev really chasse from England?"

"Is it true Krassin will soon follow?"

"What pretty hair you have, Mademoiselle, is it naturally that color? Does it curl naturally so?"

"Is there a famine in England? I hear there is no longer sugar or butter. But there will be a famine when your strike begins."

"What! you have not a mackintosh with you Nor an umbrella? Nor thicker shoes than that?"

"But do you not know there is nothing to be had in Russia?"

"You have goloshes? That is good."

"And soap? Yes, they will do your washing if you give them soap to do it with—"

Kamenev left us to attend a meeting elsewhere.

It was now pretty late, and I was very tired, the room was small, full of smoke and food. When I had finished my tea Alexandre Kamenev and the soldier who had not left us since our arrival took me back to the headquarters. I did not know what was to become of me and no one understood me. The dimly lit corridors were crowded with strange loungers. I was shown into a grim room where Lenin and Trotsky adorned the walls, and there I sat silently among people I could not talk with. After awhile to my intense relief Kamenev appeared.

In this strange milieu in which I was so utterly lost Kamenev seemed to me the oldest and the only friend I had in the world, and I metaphorically clung to him as a drowning man to a straw.

Somebody in the crowd, taking pity on my helplessness, or else wondering what I was asking for in three unknown languages, had sent him to me.

He asked what on earth I was doing there, as if I knew! I followed him to another room, bigger and fuller of people, who all looked very serious and sat in a circle. The meeting went on, and I sat obscurely in a corner wondering whether if I understood Russian, I would be allowed to be there. At last, bored by watching them and learning nothing from it, I got out a pencil and paper from the hand case I had with me and wrote a letter to Dick. It was the last place from which I could post a letter and the last time I could write letters uncensored. I wrote to Dick from my heart, thinking of him at that moment in bed, so very far away, looking so round and pink, and with one arm outside the bedclothes. Dick and Margaret both know that when I am away from them I come in spirit in the night. They often find a rose petal, or a bud, or maybe a tiny feather, something very light that I leave on the pillow to prove that I have been. Never had I been more with them in spirit than this night, when I felt so lonely and bewildered. Later on I wrote an apology to F. E. explaining why I had not turned up at Charlton to do his bust. It was one of the things that I felt rather badly about, for as I had left England the very day I was due at the Birkenheads' I could not at that time explain, and they must have thought me so very rude. It is funny that none of these people, not even Kamenev, have heard of F. E. either as Smith, Lord Birkenhead, or Lord Chancellor. Chancellor of the Exchequer they understand, but no other Chancellor.

When at last the meeting was over I was introduced to Gukofski, and gathered it was his room we were in. He is a little bent man, who broke his back sometime past in a motor accident.

He has red hair and beard, and small narrow eyes that look at one scrutinizingly and give one a shivery feeling. He asked me what my mission was, and when I told him he said, "Do you think you are going to get Lenin to sit to you?" I did think so. His eyes twinkled with merriment.

"Well you won't!" he said and chuckled.

Kamenev went off to converse on the telephone with Tchitcherin at Moscow, and did not come back. I waited and waited; Gukofski began packing a trunk; he was evidently coming with us. I watched him a man's packing is always a rather interesting and pathetic sight—but even that ceased to interest me after awhile, and I became conscious of a feeling bordering on tears and sleep.

Where on earth was Kamenev, and why didn't he come back, or else explain to me how long this waiting was to go on. After awhile I discovered that Gukofski's secretary, a young man called Gai, could speak perfectly good English. From him I learnt that our train was leaving "about midnight" for Moscow, and that I could go to it any time I liked and find my sleeper. I ought to have known this long before, it was already nearly midnight. I made Alexandre Kamenev and the soldier take me to the station immediately. Of course when I got there the train was nowhere to be found, it was in a siding. I sat down on a stone step and waited, thankful at least for the fresh air and the absence of glaring lights. When our "wagon-de-luxe" finally appeared it was the best I've ever seen, had been the Special of the Minister for Railways, and was very spacious and comfortable. As soon as Kamenev, Gukofski and his little girl joined us, the train started and we had a midnight supper of tea and caviare.

SEPTEMBER 19TH, 1920. Sunday.

All night we have journeyed and all day. It is now evening. Our special train has stopped at a wayside station for three hours to await the Petrograd train, to which we will link on for Moscow.

Then we will travel again all night and arrive at our destination to-morrow morning.

It has been a beautiful day of sunshine. I crossed the frontier riding on the engine, the front of our car has a veranda from which one can get a beautiful view. We crossed two wide rivers on temporary bridges, as the original ones lay in debris below us, having been blown up by Yudenitch in his retreat last year after his attack on Petrograd. The woods on either side of the river were full of trenches, dugouts, and barbed wire. I had tea and bread and caviare at 9 A. M. and the same thing at 3 P. M. and again at 7. There is no restaurant car, we have brought our food with us in a hamper. There are other things to eat besides caviare only I cannot eat them. There is cheese, and some ham which isn't ham I have ever known, and there is a sort of schnitzel sausage and some apples.

The soldier who was with us yesterday and is still with us, and whose name is Marinasky, is a chauffeur. I thought he was an officer. He eats with us, smokes with us, joins in the discussions and kindly lays the table for food and clears away for us. It sounds odd, but it seemed quite natural until I heard he was a chauffeur. My bourgeois bringing up is constantly having surprises!

Marinasky has a nice clear-cut face, and square jaw like the Americans one saw during the war.

This afternoon we got out of the train and walked up the line as there were three hours to dispose of. I led the way because there was a wood I wanted to go to. It was extremely pretty, and the moss sank beneath one's feet. The children collected berries and scarlet mushrooms, which they brought to me as offerings.

On the way back Kamenev and his boy and I found a dry place on pine needles, where we lay down, and to the sound of father and son talking softly in Russian I went fast asleep. The sun was setting when they woke me up. In the heart of Russia, in the company of Bolshevists, I had spent an Arcadian hour.

SEPTEMBER 20TH, 1920. Monday.

Moscow, the Kremlin.

Yesterday evening after we had started, Kamenev left us to go and talk to Zinoviev, who was on the Petrograd train, traveling also to Moscow.

Zinoviev is President of the Petrograd Soviet and also of the Third International). I did not see Kamenev again that evening, but at 2 A. M. he knocked at my door and waked me up with many apologies to tell me news he thought I would like to hear. Zinoviev had just told him that the tele-

gram announcing his arrival with me came in the middle of a Soviet Conference. It caused a good deal of amusement, but Lenin said that whatever one felt about it there was nothing to do but to give me some sittings as I had come so far for the purpose. "So Lenin has consented and I thought it was worth while to wake you up to tell you that" Kamenev was in great spirits. Zinoviev had evidently told him things he was glad to hear—especially, I gathered, no blame or censure was going to be put upon him for having failed in his mission to England.

We reached Moscow at 10:30 A. M. and I waited in the train so that Kamenev and his wife could get their tender greetings over without my presence. I watched them through the window: the greeting on one side, however, was not apparent in its tenderness. I waited, as they walked up the platform talking animatedly. Finally Mrs. Kamenev came into the compartment and shook hands with me. Mrs. Philip Snowden in her book has described her as "an amiable little lady!"

She has small brown eyes and thin lips. She looked at the remains of our breakfast on the saloon table and said querulously, "We don't live 'chic' like that in Moscow" Goodness! I thought, not even like that. There was more discussion in Russian between the two. My expressionless face watched them. I have become reconciled to not understanding.

As we left the train she said to me: "Leo Kamenev has quite forgotten about Russia—the people here will say he is a Bourgeois." Leo Kamenev spat upon the platform in the most plebeian way, I suppose to disprove this. It was extremely unlike him!

We piled into a beautiful open Rolls-Royce car and were driven full speed with a great deal of hooting through streets that were shuttered as after an air-raid. Mrs. Kamenev said to me: "It is dirty, our Moscow, isn't it?" Well, yes, one couldn't very well say it wasn't.

We came to the Kremlin; the car had a pass to get in. It is high up and dominates Moscow and consists of the main palace, some palaces, convents, monasteries, and churches encircled by a wall and towers. The sun was shining when we arrived and all the gold domes were glittering in the light. Everywhere one looked there were domes and towers.

We drove up to a side entrance under an archway, and then made our way, a solemn procession carrying luggage up endless stone stairs, and along stone corridors to the Kamenev apartments. A little peasant maid with a yellow handkerchief tied over her head ran out to greet us, and kissed Kamenev on the mouth. Then ensued the awkward moment of not being shown to any room.

After eleven days traveling one felt a longing for peace, and to be able to unpack, instead of which the Russian discussion was resumed, and I sat stupidly still with nothing to say.

For breakfast I was given coffee and an overhelping of dry tepid rice. When for a moment I found myself alone with Kamenev I asked him what was to become of me and begged him to send me to an hotel. There are no hotels, everything belongs to the Government. There are, however, guest houses, but he was averse to this as he said I would be lonely and strange. He told me to leave the matter entirely to him and he would decide in two hours.

Meanwhile I went for a walk in the Kremlin grounds with Alexandre and took a lot of photographs. The beauty of it all was a wonderment, and I was quite happy not to go outside the walls, which I could not do as I had no pass. Then I came back and waited and waited for Kamenev to come and tell me where I was to go. As the day passed by I felt more and more lonely. For lack of another book I read de Maupassant's "Yvette," but hated it and thanked God that Bolshevism had at least wiped out that vile world of idle men. At sunset I sat on the ledge of the open window and listened to the bells that were ringing from all the domes in Moscow. Below me was an avenue of trees that reached up to me with autumn colors. I thought of Dick [Clare's son] and that to-day is his birthday. I knew he must be asking, "Where is Mema, why doesn't she come? How long will she be?"

When it was dark I was still looking out and Anna Andrevna, the little maid, came in softly in her string-soled shoes and put her arms round me. She told me in broken German that I must not "traurig sein."

Kamenev came in at half-past ten. He was very tired and he precluded all further discussion by saying that it was too late to go anywhere else, and that I must stay the night. Mrs. Kamenev came in from her work a little later. She sank into a chair and drew her hand across her brow in the most approved way to betoken physical exhaustion. I was given Alexandre's room through which they have to pass to get to theirs, and I have to pass through theirs to get to the wash room, there being no washstand in my bedroom.

I suppose Alexandre slept on a sofa. Kamenev went back to his Soviet meeting at eleven, and I heard him pass through my room when he came home at 4 A. M.

I wandered about, still hynotized by the beauty of the sun-reflecting domes, and by the dead stillness which seemed a protest from the Royal stones.

Over the Tsar's palace crows pecked at the flagstaff where once the Royal standard had flown.

There is a clock in a tower at the Kremlin Gate and it has a complaining and depressing chime.

It complains once at the quarter, four times at the hour.. It seemed to say, "My people are gone! and I am sad, and I am sad—" It

45

doubtless complained when Napoleon took possession, at the Tsariste days as well, and it will always complain.

There is no satisfying some people.

I have a sort of feeling that I am staying at Versailles just after Louis XVI. My emotions and impressions are too deep, too many, and too bewildering to be measured in words.

In the evening Alexandre took me to a play at the Theatre des Arts. A big theater and well filled. The staging was very good. The play which is adapted from an old Polish legend called "Corrodine" was well acted so that without understanding a word I gathered some of the sense. In front of us sat Madame Zinoviev with a Comrad and I was glad when they talked to me in French.

It was not until afterwards that I learnt who she Was, much to my amusement, remembering that I had told her my errand, and that Zinoviev was among the heads promised to me. She asked me if I would not have to go to Petrograd to do him but I said no, that he was in Moscow at the moment, and that if I could only find a place to work in, he would sit to me at once. I wondered why she laughed.

SEPTEMBER 22nd, 1920. Moscow.

Mrs. Kamenev went to her work as usual at 10

A. M. At breakfast half an hour later Leo Borisvitch, as he is called, promised not to do any work or keep any engagement until he had taken me to my new headquarters in a guest house. We were delayed in starting by John Reed, the American Communist, who came to see him on some business; a well-built, good-looking young man, who has given up everything at home, to throw his heart and life into work here. I understand the Russian spirit, but what strange force impels an apparently normal young man from the United States? I am told by the Russians that his book, *Ten Days that Shook the World*, [the Warren Beatty movie *Reds* is based on Reed's life] is the best book on the Revolution, and that it has become a National classic and is taught in the schools.

There also arrived to waylay us a painter called Rosenfeld, who wore canvas shoes like a peasant, and kissed Kamenev on his arrival.

He offered to show me museums and things, but our only medium was German, and his was a good deal worse than mine, which was a great drawback. At midday, however, we broke free, and started off with my luggage. I bade farewell to the Kremlin and we drove across the river to a guest house on the opposite bank facing the Tsar's Palace.

The guest house is the requisitioned house of a sugar king. It is inhabited by various Foreign Office officials, also by Mr. Rothstein and an American financier, Mr. W. B. Vanderlip. A beautiful bedroom and dressing room are mine, the walls are of green damask. It looks more like a drawing room than a bedroom. The house is more or less exactly as the sugar king left it, full of a mixture of good and bad things. It is partly modern Gothic and partly German Louis XVI. The ceiling of one of the big rooms is painted by Flameng, but the best pictures (there were some Corots) have been taken to a museum.

One is extremely grateful for its comfort and hospitality, even if its taste in decoration is not of the best.

Moreover, one can enjoy it lightheartedly, for the exiled sugar king, it is rumored, had other palaces abroad, and never came to Moscow but for a few weeks in the year. He also has money invested abroad and is not in want, and can well spare his Moscow Palazzo for so good a purpose.

His old manservant waits upon us, and takes the tenderest care of the house, in the belief that the old regime will return, bringing the owners of the house with it. He says openly that he is not a Bolshevist, and takes much pride in changing our plates a great many times, and making the most of our humble fare. He insists that so far as it depends upon him we shall behave like perfect ladies and gentlemen and be treated as such.

I stayed at home all day unpacking at last, and settling down into my temporary home. Kamenev promised to come back in the course of the day, but he didn't. He telephoned, however, and arranged that I should be taken to the Ballet with the party from this house. We sat in the Foreign Office box. The Ballet was "Cophelia," beautifully produced, and the orchestra one of the finest I ever heard. The theater is the size of Covent Garden, and decorated with crimson and gold boxes all round the first tier and the house was packed throughout.

The audience consisted of working people, who had admission free through the distribution of tickets to certain unions. They were a motley crowd, chiefly en blouse. In the Royal Box, reserved for Commissars and their wives, there was a man with a cloth cap. The women were eating apples. In the box next to ours there was an old woman with a shawl over her head.

It was intensely moving to see the absorbed attention of the audience. People leant their elbows on the ledges of the boxes and watched the ballet with an almost devouring interest. There was not a cough, not a whisper. Only when Cophelia came to life as the mechanical doll, there were delicious low ripples of controlled laughter from the children.

At the ends of the acts people left the stalls to rush, not for the exits of the foyer, but to get to the front of the gangways nearest possible to the stage to see the dancers close to, and to applaud them. The people were tired people, who had worked all day and had earned a good evening and were enjoying it to the full.

My only contretemps was with a little stenographer from the Foreign Office who was in our box. She observed that I had on the red enamelled star of Communism, and that I wore white gloves. One, she said, contradicted the other the white gloves were bourgeois. I argued that it only mattered what was in my heart, and not what was on my hands. But she would not be pacified, so I removed the gloves. Considering my costume was a red tweed skirt with a red wool jersey and a tight fitting cap, I had thought that gloves would not make me over-dressed.

If my evening's pleasure was neutralized by the concentrated aroma which arose from the great unwashed, it is only fair to observe there is no soap in the country, and most people have for two years or so only had the one suit of clothes in which they stand up. No wonder—I In the car coming home I met Mr. Rothstein, who is living in the same house. I wish I could recall the abusive article I read about him in an English newspaper, but all I remember is that he is not readmitted to England. He seems to be an energetic, forceful little man. I imagine he is pretty clever. We had supper together after the theater, and conversation drifted onto that eternal comedy, the Nationalization of women. I happened to say that this had done more to harm the Bolshevik cause than almost anything and moreover that quite serious people still believed it. Mr. Rothstein interposed rather sharply, "Well a little' select circle who reads the Morning Post perhaps believe it." Is it possible, I wonder, that he is right, and that the "little select circle" do not count as much as I have all my life taken for granted they did?

SEPTEMBER 23RD, 1920. Thursday. Moscow.

I wasted a lot of time this morning trying to fix things up without the help of Kamenev. As things have turned out I might have saved myself the trouble. John Reed told me that I never would begin work unless I arranged everything for myself, and depended on no one here. On the other hand Mr. Vanderlip told me to keep calm, as his experience was that everything came in time.

Thoroughly impatient, however, I got hold of Mr. Rosenfeld who arrived simultaneously with Alexandre Kamenev and a motor. Rosenfeld took me studio hunting. The Art schools seemed to be very far away from the parts of Moscow that are familiar to me, and although every one seemed willing to help there seemed to be little to offer.

In the Academia, which I believe is only just reopening, they offered me a place to work in a gallery which obviously was not suitable. We went on to the Strogonoff school, where Mr. Konenkoff, one of their most distinguished sculptors, offered me of his best. It was like an empty kitchen, looking into a bleak courtyard. The two students who followed us round were not very sympathetic. No doubt they thought it presumptuous of me to come to Russia and expect to do Lenin! They certainly did not seem to think he would sit to me. Kamenev had warned me that most of the artists I should meet would not be Bolsheviks; probably the students I met were not, and treated me as such!

One of them, a girl, and more friendly than the rest, said to me in French: "If you are a friend of those in power I suppose you will get some food we are expected to work here all day from 9 in the morning till 6 at night without any." I asked why she did not bring her food with her, and received some jumbled explanation about rations and distribution and State Control, and no shops, which was so bewildering I avoided further discussion. It was obvious that I did not understand the condition of things and that I looked rather stupid in consequence. Another one said to me "Madame, we are waiting for deliverance. For two years we have waited. We do not know how it is to come, but we just hope that some morning we may wake up to find the nightmare is over!"

I said feebly that there had been 6 years of war, and a blockade, but I felt it was no business of mine to put up a defense for their system. I came home thoroughly depressed and disheartened, having accomplished nothing. At 10 P. M. I was sitting in the gilded drawing room with Mr. Vanderlip when the telephone rang: it was Kamenev.

He announced that he had a room for me at the Kremlin and that I must work there because all the people I had to do were there, and it was the only way to get them as they were very busy. He would send some one for me in the morning to take me there. Asked if I was lonely, resentful, or bored, and pleaded his inability to get to me owing to stress of work. Begged me to be patient and good. Promised all would come right. I went to bed feeling really better.

SEPTEMBER 24TH, 1920. Friday. Moscow.

Madame Kamenev's secretary fetched me at 10

A. M. and we found a Comrad waiting for us at the Kremlin gateway. He was a painter, young and bearded, who could speak only Russian. We got our passes to get into the big round building which used to be the Courts of Justice, and where the conferences are now held. It is the Chief Building, and the Red flag flies above it. Once inside we walked forever as it seemed, along stone corridors full of busy people. We went to the room of Comrad Unachidse, one of the most magnificent men I've ever seen, a real Maestrovic type, strong features and bushy red hair. Unfortunately he also could only speak Russian. He showed me the room which is placed at my disposal. It is big and nearly empty, semicircular in shape, with bare whitewashed walls. In one corner a formidable iron door with round peep holes in it leads into a small cell which contains a safe. The safe is sealed up with Soviet seals. The cell I was told was a disused prison. This probably accounted for the atmosphere of depression and grimness which persisted in spite of the sunlight which in the afternoon flooded my three big windows. Opposite, across the courtyard is the arsenal, and all along the arsenal walls are ranged the masses of cannon with their "N" surrounded by the laurel wreath, which leaves one in no doubt as to their origin.

While I was looking round, Kamenev turned up, he told me to make a list of my requirements, then carried me off in ,a car and was able to stay with me until 2 o'clock. These moments together snatched in between work are so rare that one almost values them. He told me I was to go to a meeting at the theater in the evening, and promised I should be in a box near the stage so that I could see well. He was to address the meeting on the subject of his visit to England. The party from our house were late in starting. We got to the theater after the meeting had begun, and were put in' the Tsar's box. This was already crammed full to overflowing, and all the chairs were occupied by Turks, Chinese, and Persians. No one attempted to offer me a place. Mr. Vanderlip and I stood for some time; people moved in and out and Turks and Persians (I shall never want to smell geranium again) pushed us about in their impatient efforts to get past or over us. All my British blood was boiling, and I realized that for the time being, at all events, I could not regard the Turks and Persians and Chinese as my brothers.

After a while Mr. Vanderlip and I were moved to the stage box. This too, was full, but not of the same kind of people. Anyway, it was nearer, and one got a better view. Clara Setkin, the German Socialist, was speaking, spitting forth venom as it sounded. The German language is not beautiful and the ferocious old soul, mopping her plain face with a large handkerchief, was not inspiring.

It sounded very hysterical and I only understood an outline of what she was saying. Then Trotsky got up, and translated her speech into Russian.

He interested me very much. He is a man with a slim, good figure, splendid fighting countenance, and his whole personality is full of force. I looked forward immensely to doing his head. There is something that ought to lend itself to a fine piece of work. The overcrowded house was as still as if it were empty. They were attentive and concentrated.

After Trotsky Mme. Kolontai spoke. She has short dark hair. Perhaps she spoke well, but of that I could not judge. Tired of standing and of not understanding I left the theater at the moment when a great many repetitions of Churchill's and Lloyd George's names were rocking the house with laughter.

SEPTEMBER 25TH, 1920. Saturday. MOSCOW.

I feel very discouraged. Every one I meet asks me what I have come to Moscow for. They assure me there is no chance of doing Lenin, especially not Dsirjinsky who is a recluse. Nevertheless, I have spent the day getting everything in order. Sackfuls of bone dry clay have been de-, livered at my door. Five men and one girl stood inert and watched me break it up with a crow bar. Finally I was able to get them all gone except one, a really intelligent carpenter, who instead of trying to talk to me, watched me and understood what I wanted. He was splendid, made three armatures for me, and then beat and stirred the clay for three hours until it was in condition. When Kamenev looked in, bringing Zinoviev, I was up to my elbows in clay, my clothes were covered, and my hair was standing on end.

Zinoviev laughed, and said it was obvious I should not be ready for him to sit to me for days, but I assured him all would be in order to-morrow, and added that a man of the carpenter's intelligence was worthy to be a government minister.

Kamenev repeated this to the carpenter, and then said to me, "Here everything is possible." Before leaving he gave me a pass into the Kremlin that will last until December, so I am independent at last, and can go in and out alone and when I please. I did not come home until I had built up two heads ready to work on. I am very tired but full of hope, remembering what I have heard that things come slowly in Russia, but they come.

SEPTEMBER 26TH, 1920. Sunday. Moscow.

I went to church with Mr. Vanderlip. We selected St. Saviour's, the big church beyond the bridge, which was built with the private money of the Tsar as a thanksgiving for deliverance from Napoleon. It has five gold domes which are a beacon to me when I am lost! A service was going on and we mingled with the crowd, which had an amazing preponderance of men. The richness of the golden and crimson robed priests seemed to throw into relief the, poverty of the people with their faces so full of sadness. What absurdly stupid things animate one's thoughts in the most precious moments: for instance, when the priest made the sign of the Cross with the three branched candlesticks in each hand, I instinctively looked to see if he had dropped candle-grease on the carpet (he had!). When the contribution plate began to circulate I watched an old peasant next to me. He drew out his pocket book, and fumbled for a few roubles, he held five of these like a cardhand, and fingered them hesitatingly.

It was obvious that he was trying to make up his mind whether he could afford to part with them all, or only with some of them. In the end he put them all into the plate, a little act of sacrifice which I am sure will not pass unblessed.

The choir singing without accompaniment was very beautiful. The masses seemed to be very fervent, one could see the Faith and Hope in all their faces. It is surely the deep religious feeling in Russia that has sustained these people through all their years of privation and prevented a greater chaos.

After church I walked along rejoicing in the sun and went to the Tretiakovskaya gallery, full of various schools of painting. Among the pictures is the famous one of Ivan the Terrible killing his son, but everything I saw was obliterated by the memory of three modern busts, the work of Konenoff, the sculptor I met at the Strogonoff school. These busts are carved out of blocks of wood. They are indescribable masterpieces, in conception, composition and carving.

I remained for some time in admiration and wonderment over this modern work. I went away after that as I could not look at anything else.

At 3 o'clock I hurried to the Kremlin as Kamenev had telephoned to me to expect Zinoviev. I waited until 4 and then he arrived, busy, tired and impatient, his overcoat slung over his shoulders as he had not had time to put his arms through the sleeves. He flung off his hat and ran his fingers through his black curly hair, which already was standing on end. He sat restlessly looking up and down, round and out and beyond: then he read his newspaper, every now and again flashing round an imperative look at me to see how it was getting on. He seemed to me an extraordinary mix-up of conflicting personalities. He has the eyes and brow of the fighting man, and the mouth of a petulant woman.

Little by little he became more tractable, and when he had finished reading we talked a little.

At moments he threw his head back and seemed to be dreaming. Then he looked like a poet. He is only 38. It is amazing how young all these revolutionaries are. I gleaned from him the news that Millerand is the new President of the French, to which he shrugged his shoulders and said it made no difference: and that the British strike fixed for to-morrow has been postponed for a week. Before he left, he said he was pleased with the start of his bust, and that I must do Lenin.

I walked home in face of a lovely sunset, the fiery ball was reflected in the gold dome of St. Saviour's. I sang as I walked, because I have begun work at last, but people looked at me.

They never looked at me before. I suppose it was peculiar to hear any one sing.

SEPTEMBER 27TH, 1920. Monday. Moscow.

Things begin to move more rapidly now, and my patience is being rewarded. To-day [Felix Edmundovich] Dsirjinsky sat to me. He is the President of the Extraordinary Commission, or as we would call it in English, the organizer of the Red Terror. He is the man

Kamenev told me so much about. He sat for an hour and a half, quite still and very silent. His eyes certainly looked as if they were bathed in tears of eternal sorrow, but his mouth smiled an indulgent kindness. His face is narrow, high-cheek-boned and sunk in. Of all his features it is his nose which seems to have the most character. It is very refined, and the delicate bloodless nostrils suggest the sensitiveness of overbreeding. He is a Pole by origin.

As I worked and watched him during that hour and a half he made a curious impression on me.

Finally overwhelmed by his quietude, I exclaimed: "How wonderful of you to sit so still." Our medium was German, which made fluent conversation between us impossible, but he answered:

"One learns patience and calm in prison."

I asked how long he was in prison. "A quarter of my life, 11 years," he answered. It was the revolution that liberated him. Obviously it is not the abstract desire for power or for a political career that has made revolutionaries of such men, but fanatical conviction of the wrongs to be righted for the cause of humanity and national progress. For this cause men of sensitive intellectuality have endured years of imprisonment.

Being Monday there is no theater, as that is the night the artists have free (on Sundays they work for the enjoyment of the people), so I dined with Mr. Vanderlip who told me many things which I may not at this juncture write down or repeat. I have not sought his confidence, so I thought it rather unjustifiable when at the end of the evening (having been a sympathetic listener) he said to me: "You know too much now, I shall see that you don't leave the country before I do."

Although he likes the people with whom he has come in business contact, he is frankly a capitalist, and glories in it. He is like the Englishman abroad who is conscious of being different to every one else, and derives from it a smug feeling of superiority. After dinner he was sent for by Tchitcherin, and I spent the evening with Michael Borodin.

Michael Markovitch, as Borodin is called, lives in our house. He is a man with shaggy black hair brushed back from his forehead, a trim beard, deep set eyes, and a face like a mask. He talks abrupt American English in a bass voice. I have not seen much of him, as he works half the day and all the night, like the other Foreign Office officials. He is usually late for meals, eats hurriedly, and leaves before we have finished. As soon as Vanderlip had gone Borodin switched out all the drawing room lights but one, that Vanderlip had put on. I asked him why he did this and he looked round the garish room and gave a slight shudder. "It is parvenu," he said, then sinking back into his chair he looked at me intently, and asked, "What is your economic position in the world?" It is the first time he has talked to me, and I found myself answering as if my life depended on my answers I Happily no one in this country knows anything about my family, bringing up, or surroundings. I have not got to live down my wasted years, I can stand on my own feet and be accepted on my own merits. Borodin mystifies me. I cannot make out when all his questions have been answered what he thinks.

SEPTEMBER 28TH, 1920. Tuesday. Moscow.

Dsirjinsky came at 10 A. M. for an hour. He is leaving Moscow for a fortnight, so I can get no more sittings, but seeing how keen I was, he stayed on and on, doling out 10 minutes and quarter hours as so much fine gold. He sits so well that two sittings are worth four of [Grigory Yevseevich] Zinoviev's.

When the Savonarola of the Revolution left, I felt a real sadness that I may never see him again.

Zinoviev sat again in the afternoon, and brought with him Bucharin and Bela Kun. They seemed to approve of Dsirjinsky's bust, and insisted on looking through all the photographs of my work.

The "Victory" is what really interests them.

I was frightfully disappointed in Bela Kun. I had imagined a romantic figure, but he looks most disreputable. Bucharin is attractive with his neat little beard and young face.

This afternoon, after all had left, three soldiers brought a gilt Louis XVI sofa and a Turkestan carpet to my workroom. These had been ordered to help to make it more habitable and dispel the severity. I had to laugh, the sofa looked so absurdly refined and out of place! I wondered whose drawing room it once furnished, and what little tea time gossips it had listened to. At that moment a sculptor called Nicholas Andreef came in and introduced himself to me, sent by Kamenev and mercifully speaking French. A big man with small laughing eyes, and a red-gray beard, typically Russian. After we had talked for awhile he described to me the difficulties with which he had tried to do Lenin in his room, while he was working. He said that portraiture was not Art.

I could but agree with him as to the difficulty always in doing portraits; that sittings are always too few and too short, but that one had to put up with it, and do the best one could, breaking one's heart over it all the time.

He said he had given up sculpture for the time being because of the difficult conditions, and had taken to drawing instead. I said that for the present I was intent on portraits, and that Art would have to wait till later. His attitude is characteristic of the sculptor species. They are all so d—d proud, and if they cannot get all the sittings they need and work under ideal conditions they do not think it worth while doing. I consider there are a few people in the world who are worth any effort to do, even if they do not give one a chance to do one's best work. Andreef laughed and said that was journalism in Art !

When I got home I found that the water had been heated for baths. This was a great joy.

I had not had one for eight days. Once a week is our allowance, and it should be on Saturdays, but something went wrong with the pipe, and we have been disappointed each evening, so that in fact I had given up hope. How one has learned to appreciate the most ordinary things that one never thought of being thankful for before. But since I have been here I have to wash in cold water; nor am I called, but I wake up quite mechanically every morning at eight. It will be wonderful to have scrambled eggs one day for breakfast, but I am getting used to just black bread and butter, and some mornings we have cheese.

I wonder a good deal about my family and friends. It is so strange to have left them without a word, and to get no letters and not to be able to write any. Mamma especially; bless her, who always says "good-night" as if it was "goodby-for-ever," I wonder what she feels about: my going off without telling her. I wonder if Papa is anxious about me, or indifferent and resentful! When I think about Dick and Margaret [Clare's daughter] I feel a sadness. I can get on without most people in the world, but not without those two, and they must wonder why they do not get letters from me. It is rather dreadful to think they might believe my silence means forgetfulness.

This evening we went to the "Coq D'or." I thought I was back in London until I looked away from the stage.

SEPTEMBER 30TH, 1920. Thursday.

Kamenev came to see me in the morning, his watch in his hand, he had 20 minutes. It was paralyzing, one cannot talk under those conditions. I confined myself to presenting him with a list of things I want done! Small wonder he comes so seldom to see me. When he does come every one in the house knows it, and one by one they come to my door and ask to see him, each wanting something of him, and his car which waits at the door is borrowed for an errand. It is very discouraging for him!

Borodin took me to Prince Igor this evening.

It combined the opera with the Ballet. In the box next to us was a party of Afghans and a Khorean with them. Down in the stalls one man was in a smoking coat and evening shirt, the first I have seen.He was very conspicuous.

OCTOBER I ST, 1920. Friday. Moscow.

Nicholas Andreef met me at the Kremlin at I o'clock. Kamenev had placed a car at our disposal for the afternoon. We went to several galleries, beginning with the Kremlin. The Palace of a Grand Duchess (opposite the big bell) has been converted into a working people's club. It was quite clean and cared for, but only the Empire

Swan furniture suggested it had ever been a private habitation. We went downstairs to a private chapel painted black and gold. This had been made into a modeling school, and there were some very good things being done from life. The Spirit of the Holy Ghost descending as a dove from above, and the golden rays of a carved sun made a strange background. My bourgeois prejudice was just for a moment shocked until I remembered that in our own old 14th century Chapel at home Papa typewrites on the altar step. It has been longer in disuse it is true, but still, one must be consistent. From there we drove in the car to the house of Ostrouckof, who showed me his room full of Ikons, some dating back to the 5th and 6th centuries. One came out of St. Sofia.

They are beautiful in design and color, and most interesting when he explained them to me. Downstairs he had a modern motley collection. He showed us a Matisse given to him by Matisse himself. It was a curious contrast after Ikons!

At 9 P. M. Kamenev came to see me to hear how I was getting on. He stayed till 11 which was very wonderful. He had had nothing to eat and I procured some tea for him and gave him some of the Crown Prince's biscuits, which are life-saving!!

OCTOBER 2nd, Saturday.' Moscow.

Hearing there was a review of troops in the Red Square at 11 o'clock, I went off to see what I could see. Every one else seemed busy, and Michael Markovitch, whom I wanted, was not to be found. If he had come with me I would have taken my kodak, but I have not a permit, and did not feel like risking a controversy alone. Arrived in the Red Square I was not allowed to get anywhere near, and I did so want to see and hear Trotsky addressing the troops. Soldiers kept the onlookers absolutely out of the square, and I stood on the steps of the wonderful church of St. Basil.

The soldiers certainly were very amiable, when I wandered rebelliously from my steps out into the road, a bayonet was leveled smilingly at me, I made a gesture of not understanding, and said helplessly in English, "Where do you want me to go?" Whereupon he laughed and allowed me to stand by his side. The crowd was very quiet and apathetic, one certainly was not near enough to get excited. In the dim distance one could hear Trotsky's voice, punctuated by cheers from the soldiers. After awhile the crowd broke forward to where I stood with the soldier, some mounted detachments came towards us, very decorative indeed with bright colored uniforms and lances with fluttering pennons. Suddenly a man at my side said to me in French: "Madame—does this please you?" I was very glad to have some one to speak to. The man was young, and though ill shaved he was well dressed in uniform. He could speak German also, but English he said he had forgotten, though he had at one time spent three months in England. Waving a hand contemptuously towards the scene before us, he said, "C'est du theatre, Madame—that is all it amounts to."

I ventured to say that a theatrical display was not much use unless there were spectators. In England I assured him we had our military pageants for the benefit of the people. What was the use of this if we were not allowed anywhere near?

He replied that it was a necessary precaution for the protection of Trotsky. I laughed, "We are three gunshots away, at least—" Then to my amazement the man began to discuss and criticize, and talk what seemed to me pure counterrevolutionary stuff. From all one has ever heard about Russian conditions (Tsariste as well as Revolutionary) it seemed to me that he was strangely indiscreet, and I asked him: "Are you not mad to talk like this in a crowd? Any one may understand French." He shrugged his shoulders: "One has lived so long now side by side with death that one has grown callous—" He then asked if I would care to go for a walk. I felt rather self-conscious of walking away in front of the crowd with a man whom they had seen me so obviously "pick-up." However in Russia there are no conventions, it was only my bourgeois blood rushing to the surface again that made it seem peculiar.

We went down to the river and leaned against the railing and talked for a long time. He was certainly very interesting and amazingly indiscreet. Happily I have nothing to reproach myself with. I adopted a perfectly good Bolshevik point of view, and argued in my usual way about wars and blockades, and urged him to have imagination and look further ahead than to-day and to-morrow. Talked about idealists, reviewed a few Tsariste items and made comparisons. But everything I said provoked him to further extreme utterances. He wished finally that he might have an opportunity of showing me "the other side."

He invited me to go to a factory with him. I asked what use that would be as I cannot speak a word of Russian. He said he would like to present to me his father and his uncle, but as they were both "known" he would have to be very careful. Finally we exchanged my name and address for his telephone number. He said that if I would telephone him to-morrow, Sunday, night, he would meet me outside my front gate at on Monday morning but he would not dare to come into the house.

At i o'clock A. M. (I have adopted the Russian habit of not going to bed!) I saw Michael Markovitch when he returned from the Commissariat, and told him about it. He said it was the queerest sort of counter-revolutionary he had ever heard of, and advised me to leave him alone.

OCTOBER 3RD, Sunday. Moscow.

I have been five days out of work. It seems much longer. I am told there are people in Moscow who have been waiting 6 months to accomplish the business they came for. Lenin seems to me further away than he did in London. There is nothing to do here unless one has work. Never could one have imagined a world in which there is absolutely no social life, and no shops; where there are no newspapers (for me) and no letters either to be received or written. There are no meals to look forward to and comfort cannot be sought in a hot bath. When one has seen all the galleries, and they are open only half a day, and some of them not every day, and when one has walked over cobblestones until one's feet ache, there is nothing to be done. One must have work to do. Perhaps I would be calmer if I had already accomplished Lenin, but my anxiety is lest I have to wait weary weeks. Return to London without his head I cannot. Michael took me for a walk; it was extremely cold. We went to St. Basil as I wanted to see it inside, but it is locked after 3 o'clock. Outside it is wonderful, painted all over in various designs and colors. I cannot understand how it stands the climate. Inside I am told it is not much to see. Napoleon stabled his horses in it. One has heard so much about Bolshevik outrages, but they have done nothing like this. Napoleon distinguished himself in several ways while he was here. For instance he ordered the destruction of the beautiful Spassky Gate of the Kremlin, the barrels of powder were placed in position and the matches were lit as the last of the French rode out. The Cossacks galloped up in time to put the matches out at the risk of their lives.

On our way home we passed by St. Saviour's church and looked in, really impelled to seek refuge from the cold. In a side chapel where the light was dim, a priest, with his long hair and beard and fine features, was preaching to a congregation which sat fervently absorbed. The heads of the women looked Eastern in their shawl swathings. I listened for some time to the strange musical tongue, of which I could not understand a word. The priest looked so amazingly like the traditional pictures of Christ that I felt I was listening to the great Master teaching in the Temple.

OCTOBER 4TH, 1920. Monday. Moscow.

When I came down to breakfast at i o my strange counter-revolutionary was sitting in the hall. How he ever got there or why he came as I had not telephoned him, I shall never understand.

I expressed my astonishment and told him I was sorry I could not go out with him, as I had some one coming to see me. I promised to telephone him later. He seemed a little disappointed, said he was "entierement a mon service" and departed.

In the dining-room I found Michael breakfasting and told him, and he got up quickly to see, but I laughed and said that naturally I had sent him away before telling any one he was there. Michael looked at me with a cold look in his eyes. He is like the others; one feels instinctively that however much they may like one as a woman, they would sacrifice one in a minute if it was necessary for the cause.

At lunch time H. G. Wells arrived from Petrograd, with his son. They are lodged in our house.

It was a great pleasure to find an old friend and to be able to talk of things and people familiar to us. He was as usual laughing and extremely humorous about the condition of life in Petrograd.

On his account we were a big party for lunch, and there was an effort to make a spread, but this was frustrated by Michael Borodin. When I asked for some of the beautiful apple cake I had seen on the side table, Michael made grimaces at me.

He had sent it back to the kitchen. The perfect Communist in him revolted against the inequality of H. G. having a special cake, considering neither Vanderlip nor Sheridan had one on their arrival!

The household call me Sheridan, like a man. One has quite lost the habit of prefixing Mr. and Mrs., in fact one cannot do it; it sounds so absurd and affected. I have not yet been honored to the extent of being called Tovarisch (Comrad) , but some people call me Clara Mortonovna (Clare, daughter of Moreton).

After lunch I went for a walk with Michael; he had tiptoed out of the room at lunch time and I asked him why. He was not very communicative, said he hated people collectively and he disliked H. G. though for no reason that I could make out. I sat far into the night, first with Michael, then with Vanderlip and finally with H. G.

We compared notes as to Petrograd and Moscow conditions. He said: "You and I do not clash. You are Moscow and I am Petrograd; it is like two different countries." But Russian habits are the same all the world over. We compared notes and laughed a good deal over the ways of life that we both experience. There is no privacy in Russian life; their rooms are like a railway station. There is not an hour of the day or night that people do not visit each other. What I experienced at the Kamenevs' he also went through at the Gorkis'. They sit up and talk till the small hours, eating and smoking till the atmosphere is thick, and then some one makes up a bed on the sofa in that room and sleeps! People come into one's room and talk while one is sitting on the edge of the bed pulling on one's stockings.

It is a condition of things that makes for great morality!

H. G. [Wells] talked to me a good deal about a Madame Benckendorff, a widow, who lives with the Gorkis and who is doing interpreter for him while he is there. I have heard of her from others. I hear she is a very beautiful and attractive woman. She has twice been imprisoned by the Bolsheviks, and is not allowed out of the country, even to Esthonia, where her children are. Nevertheless, she told H. G. that she was happier now than in the old prosperous days before the Revolution, because now life is more interesting and real!

I can think of a good many women whose lives might be considerably shaken up by the present condition of things, but I don't know if they would like it! Personally I prefer my life with all its struggles and its uncertainties since everything crashed for me, than the days of peaceful home protection and inactivity.

There is in Moscow a very charming little Madame Protopotoff, whose family used to be very rich. They had the great bell foundry and ikon factory. She has just succeeded in getting a job at the Commissariat for Foreign Affairs. A knowledge of French and German has made her invaluable in the translating department. For this work she gets not only a wage, but a food ration for herself and her mother and her child. She did not complain to me about having to work, but said it was interesting to watch the reconstruction that is going on. These are certainly wonderful days to be living in, and I think that many Russians who might have escaped have remained, to work not for the Bolshevik system, but for Russia. I have met a good many who say they could not abandon their Russia in this hour of agony and others with such Russian hearts that they could not bear to miss their Russian winter for a life of less hardship in an alien clime. These are the people to whom one should take off one's hat.

H. G. of course deplores the discomforts and the unnecessary lack of privacy. He says he simply could do no work under these conditions.

To him are absolutely necessary the morning bath, the daily papers, the quiet breakfast, and the leisure and the peace that are required to get through one's correspondence. Of course here one has neither papers nor correspondence, and that ought to give the leisure to think! But if one is so constituted that one cannot work without the start of a hot bath it is lamentable to be in Russia! Oh, H. G.—dear H. G.! I am very devoted to you, but you sadly need shaking out of your habits.

OCTOBER 5TH, MOSCOW.

H. G. had an hour's interview with Lenin. He told me he was impressed by the man and liked him. Lenin apparently told him all about the Vanderlip business, the Kamschatka concessions and the Alliance against Japan. This will greatly upset Vanderlip, who did not want the news to leave the country until he did. But I suppose Lenin's indiscretion is the indiscretion of purpose. H. G. talked to me at some length about the advisability of my going home. He too is discouraging about my prospects of doing Lenin or Trotsky. He says that Kamenev has "let me down" badly. I could only say in Kamenev's defense that he has not "let me down" yet. But H. G. had something else in the back of his head that he did not tell—I gathered he thinks there will be trouble here in a few weeks. What the conditions are in Petrograd I do not know, but here one feels as safe as a mountain and as immovable. H. G. may learn a lot of facts about schools and factories, and things, but it is only by living a life of dull routine and work, even of patient inactivity and waiting, that one absorbs the atmosphere.

Inactivity is forced upon me, I have to wait. I am waiting neither patiently nor calmly it is true, but all the while I realize that I am gaining something and that some understanding is subconsciously flowing to me. I see no danger signals. A winter of hardship and sacrifice for these people, yes, but no disorder. The machine is slowly, very slowly, working with more competence, and freedom. Of course one dislikes cold baths in cold weather, and bad food and all the discomforts to which a pampered life has made one unaccustomed, but these need not blight one's outlook. They are not necessarily indicative of a disruption.

After the Ballet "Sadko" I walked home with Michael, we had supper together of cabbage soup and tepid rice, and talked until 2 A. M. Michael always says the food is eatable even if it is not.

He never complains, he just pretends to eat it; sometimes I see his pretense! This evening he talked to me about my work. He wants me to think about a Statue interpreting the Soviet idea, and told me a good deal about the Third International, as representing a world brotherhood of workers. The plan of the Third International is very fine: "Workmen of the world unite"—if they did unite they could hold the peace of the world for ever—but unity is hard to attain. I wonder if it is not unattainable. Everything that one hears and sees here stirs the imagination my mind is seething with allegories with which to express them, but they are so big-I should have to settle for life on the side of a mountain and hew out my allegories from the mountain-side. This night in his big Gothic room I paced back and forth, my arm through Michael's, talking abstractedly, until his calmness calmed me. He knows that I have been going through a period of waiting, not unmixed with despair and anxiety. I understand so little about the Russian temperament and hear such conflicting reports that it is difficult to know what to expect. He has encouraged and cheered and tolerated me. He reminds me sometimes of Munthe, in his adhesion to his convictions, and his demand that one should live up to one's idealism.

OCTOBER 6TH, 1920. Wednesday. Moscow.

Spent the morning darning my stockings, and Mr. Vanderlip reading Rupert Brooke out loud. I was depressed to the point of resignation. It is always blackest before dawn; at 2 o'clock the Commandant of the house walked in with a telephone message: "Greetings from Comrad Kamenev and all is prepared for you to go and do Lenin in his room to-morrow from 11 till 4."

It was marvelous news. I went directly to the Kremlin with Humphries and on our way we talked about Wells and the Lenin interview, and the effect it would have on Vanderlip when he heard about it. I asked why Lenin had told about it, considering Vanderlip's business was supposed to be such a secret, and H. (who had been present at the interview) said that Rothstein (who was also present) had interposed in Russian, and asked Lenin if he was not being indiscreet. Lenin simply said that he was not and went on! I can imagine the futility of questioning Lenin as to whether he is doing the right thing! Lenin always knows what he is doing.

No one is more deliberate. With Humphries' help I got my stands and clay moved from my studio to Lenin's room. I happily had him built up, ready to work on as soon as the order should come.

OCTOBER 7TH, Thursday. Moscow.

Michael Borodin accompanied me to the Kremlin. On the way he said to me: "Just remember that you are going to do the best bit of work today that you have ever done." I was rather anxious about the conditions of the room and the light.

We went in by a special door, guarded by a sentry, and on the third floor we went through several doors and passages, each guarded. 'As I was expected, the sentries had received orders to let me pass. Finally, we went through two rooms full of women secretaries. The last room contains about five women at five tables, and they all looked at me curiously, but they knew my errand. Here Michael handed me over to a little hunchback, Lenin's private secretary, and left me.

She pointed to a white baize door and I went through. It did not latch, but merely swung behind me.

Lenin was sitting at his desk. He rose and came across the room to greet me. He has a genial manner and a kindly smile which puts one instantly at ease. He said he had heard of me from Kamenev. I apologized for having to bother him. He laughed and explained that the last sculptor had occupied his room for weeks, and that he got so bored with it that he had sworn it never should happen again. He asked how long I needed, and offered me to-day and to-morrow from i r till 4, and three or four evenings, if I could work by electric light. When I told him I worked quickly and should probably not require so much, he said laughingly that he was pleased.

My stand and things were then brought into the room by three soldiers, and I established myself on his left. It was hard work for he was lower than the clay and did not revolve, nor did he keep still. But the room was so peaceful and he on the whole took so little notice of me that I worked with great calm till 3:45 without stopping for rest or food.

During that time he had but one interview, but the telephone was of great assistance to me.

When the low buzz accompanied by the lighting up of a small electric bulb signified a telephone call, his face lost the dullness of repose and became animated and interesting. He gesticulated to the telephone as though it understood.

I remarked on the comparative stillness of his room, and he laughed. "Wait till there is a political discussion 1" he said.

Secretaries came in at intervals with letters.

He opened them, signed the empty envelope, and gave it back, a form of receipt I suppose. Some papers were brought him to sign and he signed, but whilst looking at something else instead of his signature.

I asked him why he had women secretaries. He said because all the men were at the war, and that caused us to talk of Poland. I understood that peace with Poland had been signed yesterday, but he says "No," that forces are at work trying to upset the negotiations, and that the position is very grave.

"Besides," he said, "when we have settled Poland we have got Wrangel." I asked if Wrangel was negligible, and he said that Wrangel counted quite a bit, which is a different attitude from that adopted by the other Russians I have met, who have laughed scornfully at the idea of Wrangel.

We talked about H. G. (Wells) and he said the only book of his he had read was "Joan and Peter," but that he had not read it to the end.

He liked the description at the beginning of the English intellectual bourgeois life. He admitted that he should have read, and regretted not having read some of the earlier fantastic novels about wars in the air, and the world set free. I am told that Lenin manages to get through a good deal of reading. On his desk was a volume by Chiozza Money. He asked me if I had had any trouble in getting through to his room, and I explained that Borodin had accompanied me. I then had the face to suggest that Borodin, being an extremely intelligent man, who can speak good English, would make a good Ambassador to England when there is Peace. Lenin looked at me with the most amused expression. His eyes seemed to see right through me. He then said: "That would please Monsieur Churchill! wouldn't it?" I asked if Winston was the most hated Englishman.

He shrugged his shoulders and then added something about Churchill being the man with all the force of the capitalists behind him. We argued about that, but he did not want to hear my opinion, his own being quite unshakable. He talked about Winston being my cousin. I said rather apologetically that I could not help it, and hastily informed him that I had another cousin who was a Sinn Feiner. He laughed, and said "that must be a cheerful party when you three get together." I suppose it would be cheerful, but we have never all three been together!

During these four hours he never smoked, and never even drank a cup of tea. I have never worked so long on end before, and at 3:45 I could hold out no longer. I was blind with weariness, and hunger, and said good-by. He promised to sit on the revolving stand to-morrow. If all goes well, I think I ought to be able to finish him. I do hope it is good, I think it looks more like him than any of the busts I have seen yet. He has a curious Slav face, and how ill he looks.

When I asked for news of England he offered me the three latest Daily Heralds he had, dated September 21, 22, and 23. I brought them back and we all fell upon them,—Russians and Americans alike. As for me I have spent a blissful evening reading the Irish Rebellion and the Miners Dispute, as if it were yesterday's news.

Goodness, one feels as though one had looked through a window and seen home on the horizon.

How tired I was, and I had eaten nothing from 10 A. M. and dinner was not until 9 P. M. In between I ate some of my English biscuits.

OCTOBER 8TH, Friday. Moscow.

Started work again in Lenin's room. I went by myself this time, and got past all the sentries with the pass that I had been given. I took my kodak with me, although I had not the necessary kodak permission. I put a coat over my arm which hid it.

I don't know how I got through my day. I had to work on him from afar. My real chance came when a Comrad arrived for an interview, and then for the first time Lenin sat and talked facing the window, so I was able to see his full face and in a good light.

The Comrad remained a long tithe, and conversation was very animated. Never did I see any one make so many faces. Lenin laughed and frowned, and looked thoughtful, sad, and humorous all in turn. His eyebrows twitched, sometimes they went right up, and then again they puckered together maliciously.

I watched these expressions, waited, hesitated, and then made my selection with frantic rush—it was his screwed up look. Wonderful! No one else has such a look; it is his alone. Every now and then he seemed to be conscious of my presence, and gave a piercing enigmatical look in my direction. If I had been a spy pretending not to understand Russian, I wonder whether I should have learnt interesting things. The Comrad, when he left the room, stopped and looked at my work, and said the only word that I understand which is "carascho" (it means "good"), and then said something about my having the character of the man, so I was glad.

After that Lenin consented to sit on the revolving stand. It seemed to amuse him very much. He said he never had sat so high. When I kneeled down to look at the planes from below, his face adopted an expression of surprise and embarrassment.

I laughed and asked, "Are you unaccustomed to this attitude in woman?" At that moment a secretary came in, and I cannot think why they both were so amused. They talked rapid Russian together, and laughed a good deal.

When the secretary had gone he became serious and asked me a few questions. Did I work hard in London? I said it was my life. How

70

many hours a day? An average of seven. He made no comment on this, but it seemed to satisfy him. Until then I had the feeling that although he was charming to me, he looked upon me a little resentfully as a bourgeoise. I believe he always asks people, if he does not know them, about their work and their origin, and makes up his mind about them accordingly. I showed him photographs of some of my busts and also of "Victory." He was emphatic in not liking the "Victory," his point being that I had made it too beautiful.

I protested that the sacrifice involved made victory beautiful, but he would not agree. "That is the fault of bourgeois art, it always beautifies."

I looked at him fiercely. "Do you accuse me of bourgeois art?"

"I accuse you," he answered, then held up the photograph of Dick's bust, "I do not accuse you of embellishing this, but I pray you don't embellish me."

He then looked at Winston. "Is that Churchill himself? You have embellished him." He seemed to have this on the brain.

I said: "Give me a message to take back to Winston."

He answered: "I have already sent him a message through the Delegation, and he answered it not directly, but through a bitter newspaper article, in which he said I was a most horrible creature, and that our army was an army of `puces.'

How you say puces in English? You know the French 'puces'? Yes that is it—an army of fleas.

I did not mind what he said; I was glad. It showed that my message to him had angered him."

"When will Peace come to Russia? Will a General Election bring it?" I asked.

He said, "There is no further news of a General Election, but if Lloyd George asks for an Election it will be on anti-Bolshevism, and he may win. The capitalists, the Court and the Military, all are behind him and Churchill."

I asked him if he were not mistaken in his estimate of the power and popularity of Winston and the importance and influence of the court.

He got fiery. "It is an intellectual bourgeois pose to say that the King does not count. He counts very much. He is the head of the Army.

He is the bourgeois figure-head, and he represents a great deal, and Churchill is backed by him." He was so insistent, so assured, so fierce about it that I gave up the argument.

Presently he said to me: "What does your husband think of your coming to Russia?"

I replied that my husband was killed in the war.

"In the capitalist Imperialist war?"

I said: "In France, 1915 what other war?"

"Ah, that is true," he said. "We have had so many,—the Imperialist, the civil war, and the war for self-defense."

We then discussed the wonderful spirit of self-sacrifice and patriotism with which England entered upon the war in 1914, and he wanted me to read "Le feu" and "Clarte" of Barbusse, in which that spirit and its development is so wonderfully described.

Then the telephone gave its damnable low buzzing. He looked at his watch. He had promised me fifteen minutes on the revolving stand and had given me half an hour. He got down and went to the telephone. It did not matter: I had done all I could. I had verified my measurements, and they were correct which was a relief, and so, it being 4 o'clock and I mighty hungry, I said good-by.

He was very pleased, said I had worked very quickly, called in his secretary and discussed it with her, said it was "carascho." I asked him to give orders to have it removed to my studio, Room 31. Two soldiers arrived and carried it out. I asked Lenin for his photograph, which he sent for and signed for me.

I hurried after the two panting soldiers with their load. We passed through the rooms of the astonished secretaries out into the

72

corridors, past the bored and surprised sentries, and got through to the main building. Two or three times they had to pause and deposit Lenin on the floor, to the interest of the passers by. At last he was safely in Room 31, and they returned to Lenin's room for the stands. It was a good long way and they were tired and dripping with sweat when their job was done.

To my intense embarrassment they refused money, though I offered them stacks of paper notes. They refused very amiably, but firmly. I made signs of imploration, and signs of secrecy, but they laughed and just pointed to their communist badges, and offered me their cigarettes, which were precious, being rationed.

At 4, Kamenev walked in, very surprised at Lenin being finished and already back in my room.

He had come in from a conference next door.

He went back and fetched in the Conference; eight or more men came in, some with interesting heads, others just ordinary looking workmen.

They all talked at once. One was Kalinin, whom I had seen in Lenin's room at an interview.

Kalinin is the President of the Republic, and is a peasant elected by the peasants. He was charming and promises to sit for me, but is off to the front to-night for ten days, and offered to take me with him. He told Kamenev that I worked so rapidly I could find some interesting heads there to do, especially General Budienny.

I said I thought it would be wonderful to do this work within sound of the guns. Kamenev promised to ring me at 9 o'clock to tell me if I was to start at 10. Alas! it turned out to be a troop train and not possible for a woman.

OCTOBER 9TH, 1920.

Started off in a motor with Mr. Vanderlip and some one from the Foreign Office. We went to a textile factory, a huge place and pronounced by Mr. Vanderlip to have the best and latest machinery, but there were 240 workers where there had been 2500, and there were acres of machinery lying idle, the reason being lack of fuel. Mr.

Vanderlip said that so experienced American workers could have done the work of those 240.

It is true there was a good deal of idling going on.

This may have been due either to lack of sufficient work, or to the Communist system by which each man or woman is as good as another, and there is none to boss. But what had been done was well done.

From there we went to one of the big fur stores which before the revolutions belonged to a private firm, but to-day is the property of the Government. There were rooms full of huge hampers packed with sable skins for export, and of course as I was the only woman present they dangled bunches of sable skins before me. Now sables don't say much to me if they are not made up, but silver foxes are different, and they cruelly put round my neck some silver foxes—

OCTOBER 10th, Sunday.

Kamenev came at midday to say good-by to me. He is off to the front to-morrow for an indefinite time. He brought with him a young man with close-cropped hair, and clear-cut features, calling himself Alexandre. Kamenev thinks Alexandre may be able to take care of me during his absence. I certainly need some one, as Michael Borodin goes to Madrid on Tuesday, and then what will become of me! Kamenev discussed with me about the Government buying the Russian copyright of my heads. He then asked me to make a list of the things I wanted and that he could do for me before he goes. I had several wants; for one thing I am extremely cold. The coat I arrived in is only cloth—now there is snow on the ground and the river begin-s to freeze. I have to wrap my rug round my shoulders when I go out. The peasants are far better off. They have all appeared in sheepskin coats. The fur they wear inside and the leather, which is usually stained deep orange, or rust color, is a very decorative exterior. The bourgeois women have brought out their former remains of splendor and although they may have only felt or canvas shoes on their feet, and a shawl over their heads, some of them wear coats that one would turn round to look at in Bond Street. I headed my list of requirements with the request for a coat—as well as caviare, Trotsky, and a soldier of the Red Army whom I want to model. Trotsky is expected back from the front in a few days. It is a bore that Kamenev is going away, but Alexandre promised to arrange sittings for me.

OCTOBER 11TH, 1920.

In the morning I accompanied Michael Borodin to the headquarters of the Third International. It is a beautiful house, formerly the German Embassy, and where Mirbach was murdered.

I came away in a car with Madame Balabanoff, whom I had often heard of. She is small, past middle age, crumpled up face, but intelligent. I did not find her any too amiable on our way to the Kremlin, where she dropped me.

She told me that it was absurd that any bust of Lenin or any one else should be done, her theory being that the cause not the individuals should count. The humblest person who suffers privation for the cause is equally as important as any of the legislators, she explained, and proceeded to assure me that no picture or bust of herself existed, nor ever should. Happily I had not asked her to sit for me. She practically told me that I was doing Lenin's head to take back to England to show to the idle curious. I corrected her by saying that, so far as the public was concerned, I only wished to substitute a bust for those who had him at present represented by a photograph. She was equally vehement about the photograph. Perhaps she expects to alter human nature.

Before I got out of the car, she assured me that her tirade was in no way personal and would I, please, not misunderstand her.

OCTOBER 14th, Thursday. Moscow.

Borodin found me after breakfast miserably wrapped around in my rug shivering with cold and depression. Tears were irrepressibly streaming down my face. I had several grievances which had been accumulating for some days, and at last my impatience had come to a head. The fact is I had heard of a courier having arrived yesterday from London, and no one had taken the trouble to find out if there were any letters for me. Ever since I left England on Sept. 11th I have not had one word of news, nor answers to two telegrams that Kamenev sent for me asking after the children. Secondly I had not been given the coat that Kamenev had ordered for me, so it was impossible to go out as it was too cold.

Michael for the first time seemed really moved.

He wrapped me round in his fur coat, went off to the garden and fetched up a load of wood for me I had never known him do such a thing before) and lit my fire himself. Then he telephoned to the Foreign Office. There were no letters for me, but some bundles for Kamenev—(?) He also got hold of Comrad Alexandre on the telephone to know when I was going to have the promised coat. Altogether he was very helpful, and the involuntary tears had been very efficacious. His journey to Madrid has been delayed daily. He is to start to-morrow. It seems to me that in Russia one only knows about ten minutes beforehand what one is going to do! They are divinely vague.

OCTOBER 15TH, 1920. Friday. Moscow.

I went to the Kremlin to meet Comrad Alexandre there at midday. He was to bring me a soldier as a model. Not feeling brave enough to go and review a platoon and make my own selection, I had described exactly what I wanted:

Not the bloodthirsty savage Bolshevik of English tradition, but the dreamy eyed young Slav, who knows what he is fighting for, and such as I passed every day on the parade ground. I waited in my studio impatiently till 2 o'clock, and then Alexandre arrived accompanied by a soldier who was typically neither Russian, nor military, nor intellectual, nor even fine physically. He was small, white, chetif, and had a waxed mustache. It was a bad moment. I tried to hide my disappointment and my amusement. I missed lunching in order to work on him, and began something that was not in the least like my model, but was the product of my imagination. At 5 I came home tired and hungry and cold. I lay down on my sofa and watched the dusk crawl up behind the Kremlin. At 8:30 I was called down to the telephone, which is in the kitchen. It was Borodin speaking from the Foreign Office. He said "good-by" in his abrupt manner. "This is the right way—" he said: "This is the way it should be." The maid was throwing her broom around the kitchen, making as much noise as possible, and a strange man glared at me out of the gloom. I found it difficult to concentrate my attention. Michael knows that I do not believe in "futures" but nevertheless we said "someday" and I wonder very much if that strange Communist, Revolutionary, with his mask-like face and deep voice will ever cross my path again. Tonight I regret him, but then I am lonely for the moment, friendless, and this is a place where one needs friends.

At 9 o'clock having not eaten since 10 A. M. I went downstairs to Mr. Vanderlip's room to suggest we round up some food. There to my surprise I found Litvinoff, who had been in Moscow since the day before yesterday. Our pleasure at seeing each other again was mutual and spontaneous. He is coming to stay at our house and will occupy the vacated room of Borodin.

OCTOBER 16TH, 1920. Saturday, Moscow.

Comrad Alexandre came to see me at 9 P. M. to tell me he could not arrange with Trotsky for sittings. I gathered that Trotsky had been emphatic and brusque in his refusal—but after all I have done Lenin and he is the one who counts most. I can go back to England without the head of Trotsky. I could not have gone without the head of Lenin. I have accomplished what I came for, and so—to—with Trotsky!

Alexandre said he could only stay 10 minutes, but he left at midnight. He talked Communism the whole time. Now Borodin unfurled his Communist spirit to me slowly, because he knew me, and to what I belonged, and he realized that the thing hurled at me in a crude mass would stagger me. He led me up to it with great caution. Alexandre on the other hand, with no understanding or sympathy, took all my inborn prejudices and just broke them, stamped on them, metaphorically spat on them, and gave me a big feed of unadulterated Communism. He is a fanatic, and left me breathless and wondering. All was well until we got to the children part: he said that his wife had to work, so their baby, who is six weeks' old, has to go by day to the Creche.

"Are you satisfied with the care it gets at the Creche?" I asked him. He shrugged his shoulders, said that collectively they could not receive the same attention as they could if they were cared for individually. He then volunteered the information that of course the baby was more liable to get ill and even die, if it was in the Creche, but that it was a chance, and after all his wife's life was not going to be reduced to feeding, washing, and dressing a baby. That was no sort of existence, and so what alternative was there except the Creche?

It was the cold dispassionate way in which he said it that gave me the creeps.

"What is your wife's work?" I said.

"Politics, same as me—" he said.

"Are you fond of your baby?"

"Yes—

"Is your wife fond of it?"

"Yes—

I thought to myself, she has not had to pray for a baby, and weep because the months went by. She has not had to wait and wait it is not infinitely precious to her, her baby. He then counter-questioned me:

"What did you do with your children when you became a widow and had no home?"

"My parents took them."

"And if you had had no parents who could take them, how-would you have worked?"

It is true there must be thousands of women who earn their livings and have no family in the background on whom to plant the baby. What happens in a country where there is no paternal State? In

Russia the State will clothe, feed and educate them from birth until fourteen years old.

They may go to the Creche for the day or permanently.

Children may go to the State school for the half day, whole day, or to board. Their parents may see them, or give them up for ever as they choose, and there is no difference made between the legitimate and the illegitimate child. Moreover, according to the labor laws, no woman may work for eight weeks before the baby is born, nor for eight weeks after its birth. She is sent away to a rest house in the country, always of course at the State's expense. On application she is given the necessary layette for the newborn. It is difficult to preserve one's maternal sentimentality in the face of this Communistic generosity.

OCTOBER 17TH, Sunday.

I stayed in bed all day as I felt ill, and there was nothing better to do. Litvinoff came in to see me in the afternoon and was surprised that I did not begin to work on Trotsky. I explained to him that through Comrad Alexandre, Trotsky had flatly refused to let me do him. Litvinoff could not understand this, but said he had seen Trotsky last night. It was then decided that Litvinoff would see Trotsky again during the day, and telephone to me what arrangements he could make. He then left me, to come back again in a few minutes bringing something, preciously, in both hands. It was a hen's egg. As I have not seen one since I have been in Moscow, I stifled my instinctive aversion to accepting valuable presents from men and had the egg fried for dinner.

OCTOBER 18TH, Monday. Moscow.

Trotsky's car came for me punctually at I I:30 A. M. (usually the cars that are ordered are an hour late, and people keep their appointments two hours late. Trotsky and Lenin are, I hear, the only two exceptions to the rule). I made Litvinoff come and tell the chauffeur that he was first to go to the Kremlin with me to fetch my things. When we got to the big round building in the Kremlin in which I have my studio, I took the chauffeur to the pass office and explained by signs by showing my own pass that I required one for the chauffeur. This was done. It is satisfactory to have arrived at the stage when I get a pass for some one else, instead of some one else getting one for me. Kamenev told me the other day that I walk into the Kremlin with the air of one who belonged to it.

Trotsky's chauffeur, myself, and the plaster moulder who was there working, carried the things down to the car, and I was driven to a place some way off, the War Ministry, I think. Getting in was not easy, as I had no pass, and there was an altercation with the sentry. I understood the chauffeur explaining: "Yes, yes, it's the English sculptor—" but the sentry was adamant. He shrugged his shoulders, said he didn't care, and made a blank face. I had to wait until a secretary came to fetch me. He took me upstairs, through two rooms of soldier secretaries. In the end room there was a door guarded by a sentry, and next to that door a big writing table from which some one telephoned through into the next room to know if I could come in. Unlike Lenin's room, not even secretaries go in to see Trotsky without telephoning first for permission. It was not without some trepidation, having heard how very intractable he is (and knowing his sister) * that I was ushered in, I and my modeling stand and my clay together.

I had instantly the pleasurable sensation of a room that is sympathetic,—big, well proportioned, and simple.

From behind an enormous writing table in one corner near the window came forth Trotsky. He shook hands with me, welcomingly, though without a smile, and asked if I talked French.

He offered courteously to assist me in moving my stand into the right place, and even to have his mammoth table moved into some other position if the light was not right.

The light from the two windows was certainly very bad, but although he said: "Move anything and do just whatever you like—" there was nothing one could do that would help. The room, which would have made a beautiful ballroom, loomed large and dark. There were huge white columns which got in my way and hampered the light. My heart sank at the difficulties of the situation. I looked at my man, who was bending down writing at his desk. It was impossible to see his face. I looked at him and then at my clay in despair. Then I went and knelt in front of the writing table opposite him, with my chin on his papers. He looked up from his writing and stared back, a perfectly steady unabashed stare. His look was a solemn analytical one; perhaps mine was too. After a few seconds, realizing the absurdity of our attitudes, I had to laugh, and said, "I hope you don't mind being looked at—"

"I don't mind," he said, "I have my revanche in looking at you, and it is I who gain."

He then ordered a fire to be lit because he thought it was cold for me. It was not cold, it was overheated, but the sound and sight of the fire were nice. A matronly peasant woman with a handkerchief tied round her head came and lit it. He said he liked her because she walked softly, and had a musical voice. Curious that he should admire in another what is so characteristic of himself; his voice is unusually melodious.

Seeing that he was prepared to be amiable I asked him if I could bother him with measurements. "Tout ce que vous voudrez [all you want]," he said, and pointed out to me how unsymmetrical his face is.

He opened his mouth and snapped his teeth to show me that his underjaw is crooked. As he did so, he reminded me of a snarling wolf. When he talks his face lights up and his eyes flash.

Trotsky's eyes are much talked of in Russia, and he is called "the wolf." His nose is also crooked and looks as though it had been broken. If it were straight he would have a very fine line from the forehead. Full-face he is Mephisto. His eyebrows go up, at an angle, and the lower part of his face tapers into a pointed and defiant beard.

As I measured him with calipers, he remarked:

"Vous me caressez avec des instruments d'acier." [You caress me with steel instruments.]

He talks very rapidly and very fluent French, and could easily be mistaken for a Frenchman. I dragged my modeling stand across the room to try for a better light on the other side. He watched me with a weary look, and said, "Even in clay you make me travel, and I am so tired of traveling." He explained to me that he is not as desperately busy as usual because there is Peace with Poland, and good news from the South. I told him that I had nearly gone to the Southern front with Kalinin who wanted to take me. But that Kamenev wouldn't let me go because it was a troop train. Without hesitating a moment he answered:

"Do you want to go to the front? You can come with me."

He was thoughtful for awhile, and then asked me, "Are you under the care here of our Foreign Office?"

I said I was not.

"But who are you here with? Who is responsible for you?"

"Kamenev," I said.

"But Kamenev is at the front."

"Yes."

"Then you are alone? H'm—that is very dangerous in a revolutionary country. Do you know Karahan, Tchitcherin's secretary?"

"Yes, he is living in our house, so is Litvinoff."

"Ah, Litvinoff. I will ring him up."

He did ring him up, but what he said I could not understand. Litvinoff told me later that Trotsky had asked him if I was all right and if it would be indiscreet or not to show me the Front. Litvinoff gave me a good character.

At 4 o'clock he ordered tea, and had some with me. He talked to me about himself, and of his wanderings in exile during the war, and how, finally, at the outbreak of the revolution he sailed on a neutral ship from the United States to return to Russia, how the British arrested him and took him to a Canadian concentration camp. He was detained a few months, until the Russian Government succeeded in obtaining his release.

He was particularly incensed at the British interfering with the movements of a man who was not going to Britain, nor from a British colony, nor by a British ship: "But I had a good time in that camp," he said. "There were a lot of German sailors there, and I did some propaganda work. By the time I left they were all good revolutionaries, and I still get letters from some of them."

At 5 I prepared to leave. He said I looked tired. I said I was tired from battling with my work in such a bad light. He suggested trying by electric light, and we agreed for 7 o'clock the next evening. He sent me home in his car.

OCTOBER 19TH, 1920. Moscow.

Trotsky's car came at 6:30. Nicholas Andreef had been having tea with me, and I offered to give him a lift as he lives somewhere near the War Ministry. It was snowing hard and there was a driving wind, which lifted up the frozen snow and blew it about like white smoke. The car had a hood, but no sides. In the Red Square we punctured. For some time 'we sat patiently watching the passers-by falling down on the slippery pavement, and the horsecarts struggling up the hill. Winter has come very suddenly and one month too soon. The horses have not yet been shod for the slippery roads, consequently they can hardly stand up. This morning I counted four down all at the same moment. In London a fallen horse attracts a good deal of attention, and a crowd collects—but here no one even turns his head to look. I have been much laughed at because I stop to watch, but the method of getting the horse up amuses me. The driver (man or woman, as the case may be) gets behind and pushes the cart. The horse, so weak that he has no resisting power impelled forward by the shafts, struggles to his feet in spite of himself. No unharnessing is necessary. This evening when I became too cold to be interested any longer by the passers-by falling in the Red Square, I asked the chauffeur if he had nearly finished. He answered "cichas," which literally translated is "immediately" but in practice means to-morrow, or next week!

So I pulled up the fur collar of my inadequate cloth coat, put my feet up lengthways on the seat, and let Andreef sit on them to keep them warm.

I arrived at Trotsky's at 7:30. He looked at me and then at the clock. I explained what had happened. "So that is the reason of your inexactitude," he said. An inexactitude which could not in the least inconvenience him as he did not have to wait for me. He kissed my frozen hand, and put two chairs for me by the fire, one for me and one for my feet. When I had melted and turned on all the lights of the crystal candelabra he said, "We will have an agreement, quite businesslike: I shall come and stand by the side of your work for five minutes every half hour." Of course the five minutes got very enlarged, and we talked and worked and lost all track of time. When the telephone rang he asked, "Have I your permission?" His manners are charming. I said to him: "I cannot get over it, how amiable and courteous you are. I understood you were a very disagreeable man! What am I to say to people in England when they ask me, 'What sort of a monster is Trotsky?'" With a mischievous look he said: "Tell them in England, tell them—(But I cannot tell them!) I said to him, "You are not a bit like your sister_" The shadow of a smile crossed his face, but he did not answer.

I showed him photographs of my work. He kept the ones of the "Victory." Among the portraits, he liked "Asquith" best and said that one was worked with more feeling and care than any of the others. He took for granted that Asquith must like me, which is not necessarily the case, and said half laughingly: "You have given me an idea—if Asquith comes back into office soon (there is a rumor that he might bring in a coalition with labor and recognize Russia) I will hold you as a hostage until England makes peace with us." I laughed, "What you are saying humorously is what a British Official told me seriously, only he said it apropos of Winston. As a matter of fact, I'd be proud if I could be of any use in the cause of Peace. But if you said you would shoot me, Winston would only say 'shoot,'" which is to my mind the right spirit, and exactly the spirit that prevails among the Bolsheviks.

They would not hesitate to shoot me (some of them have told me so) if it were necessary, even if they liked me as a woman. Winston is the only man I know in England who is made of the stuff that Bolsheviks are made of. He has fight, force, and fanaticism.

Towards the end of the evening, as Trotsky said nothing more about the project of my going to the Front, I asked him if he had decided to take me or not. He said: "It is for you to decide if you wish to come—but I shall not start for three or four days." It was getting late, he looked very tired. He was standing in front of the clay with his back to it so that I had the two profiles exactly in line. His eyes were shut and he swayed. For a moment I feared he was going to faint. One does not think of Trotsky as a man who faints, but anything may happen to a man who works as he does. My thought was of my work, and I said to him: "Do not fall backward, or you fall on my work." He answered quickly, "Je tombe toujours en avant!" I asked him to order the motor, having realized that unless he sends for it I have to wait outside in the cold or look for it in the garage. While the car was coming round he sent for a reproduction of a portrait of himself by an artist friend of his, to show me that the same difficulties I am having with his jaw and chin were experienced also by the draughtsman who only succeeded in this, the last of a great many sketches. It is evidently one that Trotsky likes, for it is reproduced in color in almost every office one goes into. I told him I wanted it and he wrote upon it "Tovaritsch Clare Sheridan" and signed it. This has its effect on the Bolsheviks who have been into my room and have seen it!

OCTOBER 20TH, 1920. Moscow.

Comrad Alexandre telephoned that he would fetch me at one o'clock to go to the fur store. I suppose the intense cold had at last moved either his pity or his anxiety for me. Before I left, Vanderlip said that if there was any choice, and I was fool enough not to choose a sable coat, he would never speak to me again. The threat left me unmoved. It is only on occasions of necessity when we exchange valuable presents, say a new tooth brush for a box of pills, that we have an armistice. On the way to the fur store Alexandre picked up another man, unknown but very nice, with whom I talked a mixture of English and German. We went to one of the biggest storehouses in Moscow, which like all the rest had been a private firm, but has been requisitioned by the Government. It was a cave-like building, dark and stone cold. We went up in a cage lift to what seemed to be the attic. It was low and long and dark and an arclight barely lit up the corner. Coats hung from the ceiling like so many hundred Bluebeard wives.

I took off mine to try on. An old man who looked like Moses and spoke German showed me the best and told me to make my choice. Alexandre looked on with a grim smile, and asked if I was the proverbial woman, or whether I'd make my choice within reasonable limits of time. It was not easy. The coats dated back three years, and some were even too old-fashioned for Moscow! I liked a brown Siberian pony lined with ermine, but the moth had got into the pony. I liked a broadtail but it was thin as cloth. They offered to have it furlined for me, but my need was immediate. There was a mink, but it had an antiquated flounce. There were astrachans, but every one in Moscow has astrachan, and it seemed too ordinary. I felt bewildered. My attention then wandered to a row of shubas: big sleeveless cloaks of velvet, that wrap around one, and descend to one's feet. There was a dream lined with blue fox, and another with white. My friends put one around my shoulders, it was lined with sable: light as a feather, and warm as a nest.

I despairingly voiced the fact that I could not walk about the streets of Moscow in a wine colored velvet and sable cape. They said I could, but then they were wrong. "I look much too bourgeois, I shall be shot!"

"You won't be shot, and sable is good enough for a good worker." I showed a sable stole to Alexandre and told him it was the blackest and most beautiful bit of sable one could find. He shrugged his shoulders with perfect indifference, and said he knew nothing about it. Finally I walked out in a very practical black Siberian pony lined with gray squirrel, divinely warm though rather heavy, and Alexandre said to me: "Now you can say you have shared in the Government distribution of Bourgeois property to the people."

At 7:30 P. M. Trotsky sent his car for me, but a soldier stopped us before we even reached the block where the War Ministry is. The whole bit of road was 'being especially guarded. The reason for this is because foreign papers have announced an impending counter-revolution, but if there is any such plot their warning has been given most obligingly in time, and steps have been taken to deal with it. The town is placarded with notices that inhabitants must not be out after midnight. It gave one just a small thrill and there have been none so far. This evening when I arrived Trotsky stood by the fire while I was warming and I asked him for news. He says that the German workers have voted in favor of joining the Moscow International which is very important. "England is our only real and dangerous enemy," he said. "Not France?" I asked. "No, France is just a noisy hysterical woman, making scenes: but England that is different altogether."

He talked about the persistence of the Foreign press in decrying the stability of the Soviet Government. All the Governments of Europe, he said, had undergone changes in the last three years. He pointed to France, Italy, the Central Powers, Turkey, and finally Poland. The British Government was holding out longer than any other, but that was pretty rocky, and its ministers were constantly changing their posts. The Soviet Government was the oldest Government in Europe, and the only one in which the Ministers retained their posts and displayed any unity, and this in spite of every effort on the part of the world to dislodge them!

He then busied himself at his table with papers.

I worked for an hour and we never spoke. But he never disregarded me as Lenin did. I could walk round Lenin and look at him from all sides, while he remained absorbed in his reading, and apparently oblivious of my presence. Whenever I go near Trotsky he looks up sharply from his work, with piercing eyes, and I forget which part of his face I was intent upon. Towards the end of the evening, when even my tiptoe stalking had aroused him, he asked me, "Avez nous besoin de moir?" [Do we need more?] I replied yes, as always. He came and stood by the clay but he is very critical, and watches it and me all the time, and makes me nervous. I undid and did over again a good deal.

The room was hot, and the clay got dry; it was uphill work. Never have I done any one so difficult. He is subtle and irregular. At one moment the bust looked like Scipio Africanus, and I could see he was dissatisfied; then when I had altered it and asked him what he thought, he stood for some time in silence with a suppressed smile before he let himself go: "It looks like a French Bon Bourgeois, who admires the woman who is doing him, but he has no connection with Communism!"

Happily the peasant woman came in with tea, and I sat down wearily with my head in my hands, utterly dispirited and discouraged. Only the fierce determination to make it come right roused me and I went at it again. He said as he watched me,

"When your teeth are clenched and you are fighting with your work, VOUS ites encore femme." I asked him to take off his pince-nez, as it hampered me. He hates doing this, he says he feels "desarme" and absolutely lost without them. It seemed akin to physical pain, taking them off they have become part of him and the loss of them completely changes his individuality. It is a pity, as they rather spoil an otherwise classical head.

While he was standing there helplessly with introspectively half closed eyes, he remarked on my name being spelt the same way as that of the playwright. I explained that I had married a direct descendant. He was interested and said,

"The School for Scandal" and "The Rivals," had been translated and were occasionally acted here in Russian. He then got on to Shakespeare. I wish I could recall the words in which he described his appreciation, exclaiming finally, "If England had never produced anything else, she would have justified her existence." We disagreed as to Byron and Shelley. He, like others I have met here, preferred Byron, and insisted in spite of my assertions to the contrary that Byron was the greater Revolutionary of the two. He was surprised that I loved Swinburne. He said he would have thought me too much of this world to love the spirituality of Swinburne. I said: "One has one's dreams." He gave a sigh:

"Yes," he said, "we all have our dreams."

When at the end of the evening I was dissatisfied with my work and feeling suicidal I. asked him,

"May I come back and work to-morrow night?"

"And the night after," he answered, and added, laughing, that he would rig the place up as a studio for me, and that I could do General Kamenev after I'd finished him. General Kamenev (who is no relation to Leo Kamenev) is the Commander-in-Chief and was a very distinguished Tsariste officer. I hear that he strongly warned the War Ministry against advancing too far towards Warsaw, and foretold the debacle that has since been fulfilled. But he was not listened to, perhaps because of his Tsariste tradition. Probably his opinion is more respected now. Trotsky asked me if I would like to do Tchitcherin, and I explained that never before had I worked under such difficult conditions, and that although I had made efforts for Lenin and himself I did not feel like doing it again for any one else. He was quite indignant and said, "What difficulty have you had in working here?" True it was a perfectly good room and excellent light, but Tchitcherin would not move out of his Commissariat and that would mean new conditions to adapt one's self to, nor does any one understand the difficulties of moving the finished work back to the Kremlin.

Trotsky swept my excuses aside: "Of course you must do Tchitcherin—it is almost a diplomatic obligation on his part to be done."

It was a quarter to midnight when I prepared to stop work and looked desperately at the clock:

"What about this order—how am I. to be home at midnight?" I asked. He said, "I will take you myself." At about half after midnight we left.

A man in uniform joined us and sat next to the driver. He had in his hands a very big leather holster. We started off by going in the opposite direction to the right one, and I had to try and describe to them the way. We turned back, and crossing the bridge we were stopped by five soldiers. The man with the holster had to show our papers by the light of the car lamp. It delayed us several minutes. I said to Trotsky: "Put your head out of the window and say who you are."

"Taisez-nous," said Trotsky peremptorily. I sat rebuked and silent until we were able to pass on unrecognized. He explained afterwards that he did not want them to hear a woman's voice in the car talking English. I was talking French as we always do together, and what does it matter to any one in this country whether there is a woman in a Government car or not but I did not argue.

OCTOBER 21 ST, 1920. MOSCOW.

I went to see my friend the plastermolder who is working for so many thousand roubles a day in my studio. He is making piecemolds of the busts, so that I can have duplicates when I go. I asked Andreef why he had to be paid so much. Andreef explained that he is the only moulder in Moscow, so he can ask what he likes—"He says he will work for this, and not for that." And Anclreef held a thousand rouble note in one hand, and a hundred rouble note in the other. "But it is all the same really, only it's a different pattern!" And he laughed. Certainly money has no value here, and no meaning. At 8 o'clock I went back again to the War Commissariat in Trotsky's car. On arrival I told him that I had got to get this work right to-night, and that he was not to be critical and look at it all the time and make me nervous.

He was surprised and said that he had no idea he had that effect on me, that all he wanted was to help. "Je veux travailler cela avec vous." [I want to work with this.] His criticism he said was from intense interest, and that for nothing in the world would he be discouraging. He promised, however, to be good, and offer no opinion until asked. It was a better night for work. I felt calmer and it went pretty well.

The worst difficulties were surmounted.

Trotsky stood for me in a good light and dictated to his stenographer. That was excellent.

His face was animated and his attention occupied.

I got all one side of his face done. Then came the question of the other side. He laughed, suggested another dictation, offered to stand in another position, and called back his stenographer.

When we were alone again he came and stood close beside the clay and we talked while I went on working. We talked a little about me. He said I should remain in Russia a while longer, and do some big work—something like my "Victory." "An emaciated and exhausted figure and still fighting and that is the allegory of the Soviet."

I answered him that I could get no news of my children and therefore must go back.

"I must return to my own world, to my own conventional people whose first thought is always for what the world will think. Russia with its absence of hypocrisy and pose, Russia with its big ideas, has spoilt me for my own world."

"All! that is what you say now, but when you are away—" and he hesitated.

Then suddenly turning on me, with clenched teeth and fire in his eyes, he shook a threatening finger in my face: "If when you get back to England nous nous calomniez as the rest have, I tell you I will come to England et je vous—" He did not say what he would do, but there was murder in his face.

I smiled: "That is all right. Now I know how to get you to England." (Then to fall in with his mood): "How can I go back and abuse the hospitality and the chivalrous treatment I have received?"

He said, "It is not abusing, but there are ways of criticizing even without abuse. It is easy enough here to be blinded par les saletes et les souffrances [by dirt and suffering] and to see no further than that, and people are apt to forget that there is no birth without suffering and horror, and Russia is in the throes of a great accouchement."

He talks well, he is full of imagery and his voice is beautiful.

We paused for tea, and I talked to him of things I had heard about the schools. In reply he said he had heard no adverse reports of the coeducation scheme for boys and girls. There might be an individual case of failure, though even of such a case he had not heard. He then compared the present system with that of boy colleges of his own day, and he said that his own boy of fourteen had nicer ideas about girls, and far less cynicism than he had at the same age. The boy apparently confides in his mother, so he knows something about it.

To-night he sent me home alone in his car. He excused himself, saying it was the only time it was possible for him to walk. He kissed my dirty hand and said that he would always preserve a memory of "Une femme—avec une aureole de cheveux et des mains tres sals." [A woman with messy hair and dirty hands.]

OCTOBER 22ND, 1920. Moscow.

Finished!

I worked until half after midnight. I think it is a success. He said so, but it has been such a struggle.

About half way through the evening, the electric lights went out. A secretary lit four candles. On the telephone Trotsky learnt that the lights had gone out all over the town.

I asked him hopefully if it could possibly be the outburst of a counter-revolution.

He laughed and asked if that was what I wanted.

I said I thought it would break the monotony.

Until the lights went on I read the leading article on Bolshevism in The Times of, I think, October 4th. He had several English papers on his desk and we read together with much amusement, that he (Trotsky) had been wounded, and that General Budienny has been court-martialed.

There were even descriptions of barricades in the streets of Moscow. Some one must have mistaken the stacks of fuel that the tramcars are bringing in and unloading every day. When the lights went on I worked hectically until half after midnight with the desperation of knowing it was the last sitting.

At midnight he was standing by the side of the work, rather tired and very still and patient, when suddenly I had the thought of asking him to undo his collar for me. He unbuttoned his tunic and the shirt underneath, and laid bare his neck and chest. I work like a fury for half an hour which was all too short. I tried to convey into my clay some of his energy and vitality. I worked with the concentration that always accompanies last moments. When I left he said to me,

"Eh bien, on ira ensemble au fronte?" But something tells me that we will never meet again.

I feel that it is almost worth while to preserve the impression of our hours of individual work, collaboration and quietude, silently guarded over by a sentry with fixed bayonet outside the door. To let in the light of day would be to spoil it.

There is a French saying: "On n'est pas toujours nee dans son pays." It equally follows that all are not born in their rightful sphere. Trotsky is one of these. At one time, in his youth, what was he? A Russian exile in a journalist office.

Even then I am told he was witty, but the wittiness that is bitterness. Now he has come into his own and has unconsciously developed a new individuality. He has the manner and ease of a man born to a great position. He has become a statesman, a ruler, a leader. But if Trotsky were not Trotsky, and the world had never heard of him, one would still appreciate his very brilliant mind. The reason I have found him so much more difficult to do than I expected, is on account of his triple personality. He is the cultured well read man, he is the vituperative fiery politician, he can 'be the mischievous laughing school-boy with a dimple in his cheek. All these three I have seen in turn, and had to converge them into one clay interpretation.

OCTOBER 23RD, 1920. Saturday. Moscow.

I went in the morning to fetch away the bust and take it to my room in the Kremlin. I went at Y i before Trotsky had got there. His motor was at my disposal and three men to convey the precious work away. These are the moments that take years off my life! It arrived, however, undamaged, which was little short of a triumph.

When my plaster moulder saw it he exclaimed with pleasure. Apparently it is very like, and every one is pleased. As Trotsky is adored, I take it as a great compliment to my work that the Bolsheviks consider it good enough.

The relief of having accomplished him as well as Lenin is indescribable. I wake up in the night and wonder if it is true or a dream. Now I am completely happy; I have achieved my purpose.

I have proved myself to these people, and they in return have proved their belief in me by their trouble and courteousness. I am no longer harassed by anxieties and fears. Those who discouraged me in the early days, treat me now with respect, consideration, and even admiration. I am happy, I am happy, I sing when I wake in the morning, I sing when I wash in cold water, I come down to my breakfast of black bread with a lighter step! I breakfast every morning with Litvinoff. By coming down at II the others have finished, so we can talk. If Rothstein is present the conversation becomes Russian. If Vanderlip is there he talks all the time about America. (He usually leaves the room with boredom if conversation is on any other subject!) It is the fashion in Europe to vilify Litvinoff and to regard him as a terribly dangerous man. I suppose he is an astute diplomatist. Whatever he is he is better than he pretends, and though he gets no credit for it, he has done a good deal for the British prisoners here. He has an unfortunately abrupt manner, and a way of refusing to do things, by pretending it is no concern of his, but straightway he will go off and do a kindness to the very people who are damning him for having refused. To me he is frank, outspoken, and always ready to help.

I have a great trust in him, and I know he is my friend, and will carry out his self-imposed task of protecting me. But to-day he gave me furiously to think. Suddenly, without any warning, he sat back in his chair and fixed me with his small eyes: "Do you know a man called Russel Cooke?" he asked. It was rather a surprising question, and I admitted that I knew a very young man called Sidney Russel Cooke. Though why Litvinoff should have ever heard of him I couldn't imagine. He went on to say that Kamenev knows him. I said yes, that Kamenev had met him through me. Litvinoff said: "He is in the British Intelligence Service, isn't he?" I confess to a slight shiver down my spine when he said this; but I refuted the statement. I said that so far as I knew (and it hadn't interested me very much)

Sidney Cooke was working in the city awaiting a propitious moment to plunge into rather liberal politics. Litvinoff gave a sort of grunt, which denoted nothing at all, and refused to be drawn any further on the subject. But something seems to be in the air, and I cannot tell what it is. Odd things happen, quite small things, but they give one a feeling of insecurity. I have asked if I may see Constantin Benckendorff.* I have explained that he is the only friend I've got in Russia, and that I haven't seen him since before I married.

When I return to England I shall see his mother and sister, and would like to give them news of him. Litvinoff said that Benckendorff was, he thought, at Riga, but he would find out. Later he came to me, and said rather mysteriously:

"Don't try to see your friend Benckendorff, and please don't ask me why, but be advised by me, not to ask any one to arrange for you to see him."

So there it is. I do not understand, but one has learnt not to argue, and, moreover, to do as one is told. When I said to Kamenev: "There is no liberty here," he laughed and said there is "une liberté dicipline"—and I suppose (it is hard to believe! I have become well disciplined!

OCTOBER 24TH, 1920. Sunday. Moscow.

We have all been very much saddened by the death from typhus of John Reed, the American Communist. Every one liked him and his wife.

Louise Bryant, the War Correspondent. She is quite young and had only recently joined him. He had been here two years, and Mrs. Reed, unable to obtain a passport, finally came in through Murmansk. Everything possible was done for him, but of course there are no medicaments here; the hospitals are cruelly short of necessities. He should not have died, but he was one of those young strong men impatient of illness, and in the early stages he would not take care of himself.

95

I attended his funeral. It is the first funeral without a religious service that I have ever seen.

It did not seem to strike any one else as peculiar, but it was to me. His coffin stood for some days in the Trades Union Hall, the walls of which are covered with huge revolutionary cartoons in marvelously bright decorative coloring. We all assembled in that hall. The coffin stood on a dais and was covered with flowers. As a bit of staging it was very effective, but I saw when they were being carried out that most of the wreaths were made of tin flowers painted. I suppose they did service for each Revolutionary burial.

There was a great crowd, but people talked very low. I noticed a Christ-like man with long fair curly hair, and a fair beard and clear blue eyes; he was quite young. I asked who he was.

No one seemed to know: "An artist of sorts," some one suggested. Not all the people with wonderful heads are wonderful people. Mr. Rothstein and I followed the procession to the grave, accompanied by a band playing a Funeral March that I had never heard before. Whenever that Funeral March struck up (and it had a tedious refrain) every one uncovered—it seemed to be the only thing they uncovered for. We passed across the Place de la Revolution, and through the sacred gate to the Red Square. He was buried under the Kremlin wall next to all the Revolutionaries, his Comrads. As a background to his grave was a large Red banner nailed upon the wall with the letters in gold "The leaders die, but the cause lives on."

When I was first told this was the burying ground of the Revolutionaries I looked in vain for graves—and I saw only a quarter of a mile or so of green grassy bank. There was not a memorial, a headstone or a sign, not even an individual mound. The Communist ideal seemed to have been realized at last: the Equality, unattainable in life, the equality for which Christ died, had been realizable only in death.

A large crowd assembled for John Reed's burial and the occasion was one for speeches. Bucharin and Madame Kolontai both spoke. There were speeches in English, French, German and Russian.

It took a very long time, and a mixture of rain and snow was falling. Although the poor widow fainted, her friends did not take her away. It was extremely painful to see this white-faced unconscious woman lying back on the supporting arm of a Foreign Office official, more interested in the speeches than in the human agony.

The faces of the crowd around betrayed neither sympathy nor interest, they looked on unmoved.

I could not get to her, as I was outside the ring of soldiers who stood guard nearly shoulder to shoulder.

I marvel continuously at the blank faces of the Russian people. In France or Italy one knows that in moments of sorrow the people are deeply moved, their arms go round one, and their sympathy is overwhelming. They cry with our sorrows, they laugh with our joys. But Russia seems numb. I wonder if it has always been so, or whether the people have lived through years of such horror that they have become insensible to pain.

Happily no salute was fired. The last time the machine guns rattled at a burial I heard them in my studio, which is just the other side of the wall. On that occasion, the old porter who takes care of me at the Kremlin, told me that his wife nearly died of heart failure. She thought "the Whites" had come. Probably it affects other jumpy people in the same way. Here the terror of the Whites is as great as on the other side the terror of the Reds! The poor people don't want any more fighting. I think they are quite indifferent as to who rules them, only they want Peace.

When I got back I found Maxim Litvinoff who also had been at the funeral and had looked for me in the crowd in vain. He says he has arranged with Tchitcherin that I am to begin him on the morrow. I have not asked to do him, but if it is all arranged for me I am only too delighted.

But I do not look forward to working at the Commissariat for Foreign Affairs. It is the Hotel Metropole, in the Place de la Revolution, and although it will not be necessary to have a pass, and there will be none of the sentry difficulties, as with Lenin and

Trotsky, the drain smells are such that one climbs the stairs two at a time holding one's breath I There are bits of the Kremlin that are enough to kill the healthiest person, but the Metropole baffles all description. Inside the offices it is all right, but the double windows everywhere are hermetically sealed for the winter, and I' wonder that people do not die like flies. Litvinoff tells me that a new building is almost ready and that the next time I come to Moscow there will be a beautiful Commissariat. It is curious that Moscow having been one of the richest cities in the world, more full of rich merchants than almost any other, that something more was not done for sanitation. Last year owing to lack of fuel most of their pipes burst in the town. No wonder there was an epidemic of typhus. This year things are better organized, and if there is Peace on the two fronts conditions may be enormously improved.

This evening Comrad Alexandre took me to a play. He gave me my choice, and I decided that "La fille de Madame Angot," being an operette would be more amusing than "Twelfth Night" in Russian. It was at the Theatre des Arts, where Chekhov's plays used to be produced. Chekhov is no longer acted—he wrote for a class that is temporarily extinct—the workers and peasants would not understand it. Afterwards, coming home in the motor I noticed a tremendous glare in the sky. It obviously meant a fire, and I insisted on going to look for it. If the fire, when found, was disappointing, at least the search for it was interesting, and revealed to me the unsuspected size of Moscow. We drove through miles of deserted streets, where we met only a few soldiers wearily trudging through the mud. We shouted to them:

"Tovarisch! where is the fire?" There is something very pleasant in hailing a complete stranger as a Comrad—one feels at once a link of friendship. The Tovarisch, however, only waved vaguely onwards, which is the only instruction one ever gets in Moscow when one asks the way! On we bumped and jolted and skidded. There was an icy wind blowing and we had no rug. We seemed to cross two rivers, or they may have been river branches. Everything looked very beautiful in the twilight. There was no parapet to the river edge, only some tortuous tree stems; finally we arrived upon the scene. It was to find that some building in a big clearing had burnt to the foundations, and was still burning brightly. Having got out of the car and waded through the mud I could not get anywhere near, and I abandoned the quest.

A party of men returning from the fire, surprised at our having a motor, asked Alexandre for his identification papers. Happily he is a member of the Communist party. On the way home he was anxious, lest the bad road should cause some damage to the car. If it broke down, he explained cheerfully, there was no other car to be had in these parts, and no telephone to call one up, and too far to walk home. It was snowing and we got back at I A. M. after losing the way many times.

In the hall I was met by Litvinoff, who while I was having supper told me he had a message from Trotsky who asked if I would be ready to go off to the front on the morrow at 4 P. M. I had to make up my mind. We discussed the plan in all its aspects. Litvinoff was splendid, he advised me neither way, he merely said he would make all arrangements if I decided to go. I knew that going would involve cold and discomfort and I guessed I would not really see much of the front, and as the only woman I would be most conspicuous. Yet... what a temptation. Finally about 3 A. M. for various reasons I decided to preserve Trotsky as a memory. Then for the first time Litvinoff said, "I am so glad..."

OCTOBER 25TH. Moscow.

Litvinoff was most kind and helped me to move my clay and stand from the Kremlin to the Foreign Office. I would have liked a snapshot of our procession—the moulder carrying the clay block, Litvinoff, in his fur-lined coat and sealskin cap armed with the modeling stand, and I following with the bucket of clay and cloths.

On arrival at the Foreign Office we were greeted by the Chinese General in uniform and all his staff. Litvinoff, who is likely to be the Soviet representative in China, was rather taken aback by this rencontre and the Chinese enormously amused.

Later, at 9 P. M. I returned with Litvinoff to Tchitcherin's office to begin work. While Litvinoff went inside I waited in the secretary's room, and while I was waiting a man hurried through the office. He was a little man in brown trousers and a coat which did not match. With small steps he shuffled hurriedly along. It might have been a night watchman. It was Tchitcherin.

Still I waited, and the length of my wait began to annoy me, and then I began to feel something was wrong. Presently Litvinoff called me, but I got no further than the doorway.

There Tchitcherin confronted me, and in hurried and confused tones said, "To-night is impossible, quite, quite impossible..." and disappeared. He had not even allowed me to cross his threshold.

Litvinoff and I looked at each other and walked out. We went upstairs to Litvinoff's office. He was obviously upset and at a perfect loss to explain or excuse. I sat and talked until the car arrived to take me home, and from what Litvinoff said and from what I had seen in that flash I have learned something of the personality of Tchitcherin.

He is an abnormal man, living month after month in that Foreign Office with closed windows and never going out. He insists on having a bedroom there, as he says he has not time to go home to sleep. He works all night, and if a telegram comes in the day he has to be awakened.

His nights are days and his days are not entirely nights. He has no idea of time and does not realize that other people live differently. He will ring up a Comrad on the telephone at 3 or 4 in the morning for the most trivial information.

He does all his own work, and will not ring for a secretary or messenger, but runs himself with papers to other departments. He lives on his nerves and the slightest thing throws him off his pivot.

I had been told he was an angel and a saint.

What I found was a fluttering and agitated bird.

The joke is that he is looked upon as the "gentleman" of the party. He is by origin well born and propertied. His property he gave away to the people. To-day was a particularly unfortunate one for me. It happened to be the first day in months that Tchitcherin had gone out. He went to the dentist. Some one watching him from an office window described to me the phenomenon of Tchitcherin in the street. He did not go in a car, but on foot. He stood at the corner of the curb, looked at the street hesitatingly, much as one might look into a river on a cold day before plunging in. When he did finally decide to get across he got half way and then ran back. What with the traffic, the fresh air, and the dentist, it must have been a thoroughly unnerving day for him, and no wonder he received me so ill.

OCTOBER 26TH, Moscow.

Tchitcherin sent me a message through Litvinoff inviting me to do him at 4 in the morning, as this is his quietest time, but it is unfortunately my quietest time too.

OCTOBER 29TH, Friday. Moscow.

I have had 4 inactive days, but the sense of work completed is a great relief. I have drifted about with Andreef and in his spare moments with Maxim Litvinoff. On his way to work at midday he first takes me in his car to the place I want to photograph. At 5 o'clock 'he comes back and has tea with me, brings his portfolio and works in my room till 7. Then he starts out again to meetings. I have interesting talks with him, and learn a good deal. He smiles tolerantly when my bourgeois breeding breaks out. But he says I am getting better. Even Rothstein has grown to treat me more seriously.

To-day my fourth day of rest began to rouse in me a fresh energy. I long to fill in this interim of waiting with some new work. I have offered to do Litvinoff, and he suggests that I work in his office. This is so difficult that I have asked him to let me do it at home, in odd moments when he is free. Between the two nothing gets decided.

Meanwhile the sentries at the Kremlin gate have fired my enthusiasm. They are magnificent, wrapped around in goat skin coats with collars that envelop their entire heads. My efforts to get such an one to sit to me has at last been successful.

Andreef and I wandered from building to building this morning to accomplish this purpose.

Andreef is great fun to explore with. He has a "Je m' en fichiste" air, opens all the doors he comes to, and walks in everywhere. I see all sorts of places that I would never dare to investigate alone.

We walked boldly into the barracks. I dtoubt if a woman had been in before, but I did not attract much attention. A few soldiers gathered round us to hear our explanation to the officer in charge.

One or two smiled, the rest looked at me blankly!

What Andreef said of course I don't know, except I understood the officer to ask if we were Bolshevik. Apparently if we were not Bolsheviks we must get permission from the Commandant of the Kremlin before a soldier could be sent to me.

Off we went in search of the Commandant. Oh! the dark passages, and the stuffy offices. They smelt as if the air belonged to bygone ages. I am sure no fresh air ever leaks in. From there to the military store to obtain an overcoat. They lent me a new one. It was an enormous goatskin. More smells! No living goat ever could have smelt stronger. Andreef staggering under the weight and the unwieldy size, carried it to my studio to await the soldier's arrival to-morrow.

The room reeks of it. My idea is a statuette, only in Russia one could find such a silhouette.

It was still early and I did not want to go home, so we wandered to the Palace, opened more doors, and after a little conversation with some men in an office, one of them took us to see the Museum and the Armory. This was a great revelation, and I regretted not having seen it before, so that I could have had time to go often again. Our guide spoke French, and knew all the things intimately. He talked of them with pride and almost with love. The things were beautifully arranged. There were glass cases full of Romanoff crowns, jewel studded, and scepters, and harness and trappings set with precious stones. One really got quite bewildered by the dazzlement of them.

The armor is very fine, I believe, but that I know nothing about and it does not interest me. What I loved were the old coaches. There was one given by Queen Elizabeth of England, the most beautiful bit of painted Jacobean carving I have ever seen. The French Louis XV and XVI coaches looked vulgar next to it. There was a room full of silver and gold cups. I believe this contains the finest collection of English Charles II silver in the world. Moreover so many chalices had been collected recently from the Churches that there were long wooden trestles covered with these, and they were in process of being catalogued. In the furthest room were exhibited all the old costumes, Church vestments, and beautiful brocades. The Coronation robe of Catherine the Great was there, and others that had been wedding and Coronation robes of various other Czarinas. It is wonderful that these things have remained unhurt throughout the Revolution.

OCTOBER 30TH. MOSCOW.

It is acutely cold. The river is completely frozen over. Children skate and toboggan everywhere. The sidewalks have become slides, and are very difficult for the pedestrian who is not equipped with skates. Children here seem to be born able to skate. They strap them on to any kind of foot-gear, even on to big loose, felt boots, and they skate everywhere at breakneck speed.

It is a relief not to see people wearily carrying their bundles over their shoulders. Now every one seems to have put his burdens on to a little wooden sledge, and grown up people look like big children pulling toys on the end of strings. I have borrowed clothes and Jaegers from my friends. One's nostrils freeze and the breath crystallizes on one's fur collar.

The town with its white pall is indescribably beautiful. At dusk the sky is darkened by a flight of gray-backed crows. They settle on the bare tree branches with the effect of great black leaves silhouetted against a colored evening sky.

At 8:30 this evening Kamenev unexpectedly walked into my room. It is nearly three weeks since he went to the front. He was in tremendous spirits, much thinner, quite unshaved and his hair long! He was interesting about the spirit of the Red Army. He says they are wonderfully enthusiastic and anxious to finish Wrangel, and have peace. It is just possible there may be a big "coup" which would obviate a winter campaign.

More than ever do I regret not going with Trotsky. They met at Karkof and I could have come back with Kamenev.

OCTOBER 31ST. Moscow.

I went to the Kremlin and tried to work on my soldier who came to sit to me, but the clay gets so cold and my fingers so numbed, I find I cannot do anything. I build up such a big fire in the stove to keep myself warm that the unfortunate soldier in the overcoat gets nearly apoplectic.

Moreover, the hot goatskin smells stronger and stronger. Even the soldier seems to be affected by it. We cannot open the windows and let the cold in. These conditions make work very discouraging. Andreef fetched me at 12:30 and we went to the House of Shuken, who was a cotton king, and who had the biggest collection of modern French pictures that exists. It is now taken over by the Government and opened several days a week to the public. Madame Shuken is I believe allowed to occupy her rooms in the house. There is no such modern collection in France. There were represented all the artists I have been wanting to see. The first room was mostly full of Claude Monet, and there were three little Whistlers in the doorway leading to a room full of Degas, Renoir, and Cezanne.

To-day for the first time, I can appreciate Matisse; there were twenty-one in a room. Next to this was another room, with twenty Gauguins. In a further gallery there was a motley collection including a couple of Brangwyns which held their own well. There was also the big William Morris tapestry of Burne-Jones' "Nativity" which one could hardly bear to look at after the modern French.

Coming out, we passed by a rudely painted doorway in the snow painted in blotches of green and yellow. A sentry stood by. I pointed it out to Andreef who agreed that it was pure Matisse.

One has but to borrow the eyes of another and the same old world appears quite different. I remember when I had been in Florence a few days, every one looked like a Madonna!

This evening Litvinoff gave a banquet for the departing Chinese General. It was a great event.

The dishes as they appeared were like things we have seen in dreams. The party consisted, besides the General and three of his staff, of two interpreters (one being the professor of Chinese at the University of Petrograd) , Tchitcherin, Karahan, his secretary, Mrs. Karahan, Vanderlip, Rothstein and myself.

We were invited for 9 P. M., but it was half past eleven before we began, true Russian fashion, two hours and a half late. It was for Tchitcherin we had to wait; he has no idea of time.

The hours preceding were rather tedious, as conversation through an interpreter is not a success. One Chinaman talked French. He was the President of the Union of Chinese Workers.

Karahan is Armenian. He speaks some strange Eastern language, but nothing that I understand.

His wife can talk only Russian. They live in our house but one seldom sees them. They have their meals in their own apartments. He is very beautiful, his face is like carved ivory. He is a great mystery, he lives in a better way than any one else, smokes the best cigars, drives to his office in a limousine, and looks like the most prosperous gentleman in Europe in his astrachan coat and hat. He must do some very good work for the Government, or he would not be tolerated. I believe Lenin once asked what was the use of him, and he was told that Karahan was most important. Was he not the only man amongst them who could wear evening clothes?

At dinner I sat between the President of the Union of Chinese Workers and Litvinoff, who did host extremely well and was clever in placing us all. He created so many places of honor that every one was gratified. He put Tchitcherin at the head of the table so that the General and Vanderlip on either side of him felt they were guests of honor. He put me one side of him and Mrs. Karahan at the end of the table opposite Tchitcherin.

I ate so many excellent hors d'oeuvres, thinking I was never going to eat again and that nothing else was coming, that I had little room left for anything else. It was a joy even to look at a fresh salad and cauliflower.

Our old man servant was awfully happy. He had on a collar and tie and was washed, and had organized everything beautifully. He had got out the Sevres salt-cellars and the cut-glass decanters and I suppose he just felt he was back in the old pre-Revolution days and serving his master's friends. He took intense pride in it all.

We had our jokes with him as he went by.

Handing me a dish of bceuf a la mode, he said, "magnifique!" Litvinoff was reprimanded by him for using his knife for his vegetables, and was told he would not get another. When the apple dumplings came round I was done. I said to the old man, "Zafter" (to-morrow). I do hope we get some remains. I asked Litvinoff where all the food had come from. He explained to me that there is some food to be had but that the best is sent to the hospitals and the children.

Then followed speeches. Anything more deplorable to listen to without understanding than Russian being translated into Chinese and vice versa is hard to imagine. Tchitcherin spoke for quite a long time. The Chinese General's face was immovable. After the professor had translated, the General replied with much the same sort of face.

After dinner we adjourned to the Karahans' big rooms opposite. Tchitcherin was evidently embarrassed at meeting me again. I had no feeling on the subject, and merely laughed.

I said jokingly, "Comrad Tchitcherin, you have treated me very badly."

He was again quite flustered.

Litvinoff told me apropos of Tchitcherin that he had advised him to get some one extra into his office to help to get his papers straight. Tchitcherin agreed, and said that he had already heard of a young man who would do very well because "he works during the day, so he is free at night."

Litvinoff asked when the man should sleep. Tchitcherin looked surprised; he had forgotten about that!

NOVEMBER 2ND, 1920.

Felt ill. Symptoms of abdominal typhus. Panic on the part of my friends. They say they do not want to lay my body under the Kremlin wall. If they do, I have told them I don't mind speeches, but would like a prayer. The answer to that was,

"Are you really croyante?"

"Well," I said, "there are two children praying every night that I may return safe and soon, and the thought of that gives me a certain security."

"What! you teach your children to pray?"

"But surely they must have something to guide them as they start life?"

"You should teach them reality, and not fantasy."

"It is not fantasy to believe in a Divine power."

"You should believe only in your own power."

That is a conversation I have had as a result of my slight indisposition. It was a conversation that confirms the general idea I have met in others since I have been here. I know these men are idealists and selfless. I did not know these qualities could go hand in hand with atheism.

On this point Litvinoff corrected me. He did not even want to be regarded as an idealist. That was too unpractical. "We are idealistic materialists," he said. To prove their tolerance of religious thought, the churches are all open. But to enter the sacred gateway which leads to the Red Square it was necessary in pre-Revolutionary days for men to pass uncovered. A tablet has now been inserted in the wall engraved with the inscription, "Religion is the opiate of the people."

Hardly ever have I passed that by without having it pointed out to me with great pride. I never quite understood the spirit of it.

And as for the people, they seem to disregard it, to judge by the many who cross themselves as they pass. The shrine seems to be always full of devotees, who pause to pray. The religious feeling of the people will not easily be obliterated and after all, they need all the comfort and hope they can get, even if the intellectuals do not.

My stay in Russia is nearing its end. Already I see my departure in the near distance. People at home will think I am a Bolshevist, on account of my associations, but I am much too humble to pretend I understand anything about it.

The more I hear, the clearer it seems to me that economics are the basis of all these arguments, and when it is a question of political economy something happens to my mind, just as it used to when I was a child and had to learn arithmetic. A Bolshevist who can be defeated by argument is not worthy of the name. Therefore I am not a Bolshevist.

But I have tried to understand the spirit of Communism and it interests me overwhelmingly.

There are little incidents I like to recall that contribute in no way to lessen my love of the people.

As for instance, when the weather began to get cold before Borodin went away, and unable to explain in Russian what I wanted, I went myself to the back garden to fetch an armload of logs for my fire.

I had to make a long journey through the kitchen down the corridors and finally through the drawing room. I have never minded carrying my own wood, but I did think that the two men Borodin, who was telephoning, and Boris, who was idling in a Louis XVI chair, as I passed through the drawing room, might have opened the doors for me.

Because they did not, I most unforgivably lost my temper, and said I was glad I was an English woman, and not a Russian man. The effect of my attack was different on each of them.

Boris said, "But it is quite right you should carry your own wood. Communism means each should help himself."

I replied that that was nothing new, that selfhelp was the oldest deep-rooted feeling in the world and that if Communism wanted to be original it must teach the doctrine of helping the other.

Borodin followed me to my room in a state of apology and distress. He brought me two apples and a cigarette, and told me that if I peeled the birch bark off the logs, it made an excellent substitute for kindling. With his advice he did much to help me light my fire. I have never quite made out in my own mind if they were typically Russian or typically Communist. I am still wondering.

I was much laughed at once because I made Vanderlip in the street shoulder a woman's burden and carry it for her to the woman's house. She was a frail well-dressed woman, obviously exhausted by a long walk over cobblestones, and was utterly incompetent to carry the bundle containing her rations. I would have taken it for her myself if I had been alone, but as Vanderlip was champion-in-chief of the frail and the welldressed, I thought he might as well do it. Litvinoff was awfully amused when he heard about it, and said that Vanderlip might really find a good deal of work to do in Moscow on those lines.

Vanderlip one day told me with great concern that a weak little bourgeoise friend of his, once rich, but now a stenographer, had received a paper ordering her to enlist her services among those who are to shovel the street clear of snow in front of their doors.

"Terrible," he said.

"Why terrible?" I asked.

"Terrible that a woman, well-bred, and unused to manual labor, should be called upon to shovel snow."

"But," I argued, "she had better food and care when young than the working classes, and ought, therefore, to be physically stronger and more able to do this work than many another."

(I thought of some of my friends in England a year ago in the strike who made most efficient railway porters.)

I said I would take pride if I were a Russian bourgeoise in showing people here that I could do as good a day's work as any one else, and that I was not useless and helpless as they imagined.

Vanderlip disagreed. He said (and I wonder if it is the American point of view) that women ought not to work at all; they ought to be worked for.

It was quite useless to talk to him about cooperation or the economic independence of women. Besides, it was not about women, it was about Communism that I wanted to talk.

Vanderlip is a source of some merriment to the Communists. He has discovered a shop in Moscow that is allowed to sell the only remaining things the government has not requisitioned. They are birds of paradise. He has bought yellow ones, black ones, and white ones of every conceivable description. He has 'written checks for more roubles than the Soviet Bank can find notes for.

Rumor says he will have to wait three weeks until they print more notes. All Moscow has heard of the purchase. It seems to me to be emblematical of all he stands for, and of all the women "who do not work, but are worked for," who will receive them.

How long and how rambling this is as the result of no occupation and an enforced stay within doors. It is useless to write letters home, and this is a sort of unburdening. I often wonder about my family— whether they are anxious about me knowing nothing of the peaceful truth), or whether they are too disapproving to be anxious.

I love the bedrock of things, here, and the vital energy. If I had no children I would remain and work. There may be no food for the body, but there is plenty of food for the soul, and I would rather live in discomfort in an atmosphere of gigantic effort, than in luxury among the purposeless. I find I no longer dream of home, and have grown used to conditions which at first seemed hard. I am thankful for the peace which I once mistook for dullness, and appreciate the absence of all the petty tyrannies of civilized life.

My mode of living suits me very well. I am glad not to have to take any part in the management of a house. I prefer bad food than being consulted about it. What the housemaid breaks is not mine, nor any concern of mine. There are no boredoms such as gas bills, taxes, rent and rates, or Income Tax returns. I never have to sign a check, nor go out with a purse. The obliteration of all social life is a boon. There are no invitations by telephone to accept, refuse, or make decisions about. There is no perplexity about the choice of apparel, nor letters by post that have to be answered. There is leisure to read, leisure to think, leisure to observe. The big ideas, wide horizons and destruction of all the conventions have taken hold of me. Of course I realize that as a guest of the government I am judging things from a personal point of view, and not the point of view of the Russian people. (Few of us are big enough to be purely impersonal.) I like living in this way. It may seem a strange taste to those people who have the sense of possession, the collectors' instinct, or the need of a fixed home. I have none of these. So long as I have a place to work in, and plenty of work to do, and leisure in which to think about it I ask little more.

My ear has accustomed itself to the language of Communism, I have forgotten the English of my own world. I do not mean that I am a Communist, nor that I think it is a practical theory, but it seems to me, nevertheless, that the Russian people get a good many privileges gratis, such as education, lodging, food, railways, theaters, even postage, and a standard wage thrown in. If the absence of prosperity is marked, the absence of poverty is remarkable. The people's sufferings are chiefly caused by lack of food, fuel and clothing. This is not the fault of the Government. The Soviet system does not do it to spite them, or because it enjoys their discomfiture.

Only Peace with the world can ameliorate their sufferings, and Russia is not at war with the world, the world is at war with Russia. Why am I happy here shut off from all I belong to? What is there about this country that has always made every one fall under its spell? I have been wondering. My mind conjures up English life and English conditions, and makes comparisons. Why are these people who have less education so much more cultured than we are? The galleries of London are empty. In the British Museum one meets an occasional German student. Here the galleries and museums are full of working people. London provides revues and plays of humiliating mediocrity, which the educated classes enjoy and applaud. Here the masses crowd to see Shakespeare. At Covent Garden it is the gallery that cares for music, and the boxes are full of weary fashion, who arrive late and talk all the time.

Here the houses are overcrowded with workers, and peasants who listen to the most classical operas. Have they only gone as some one might with a new sense of possession to inspect a property they have suddenly inherited? Or have they a true love of the beautiful, and a real power of discrimination? These are the questions I ask myself. Civilization has put on so many garments that one has trouble in getting down to reality.

One needs to throw off civilization and begin anew, and begin better, and all it needs is just courage.

What Lenin thinks about nations applies to individuals. Before reconstruction can take place there must be a Revolution to obliterate everything in one that existed before. I am appalled by the realization of my upbringing and futile viewpoint instilled in me by an obsolete class tradition.

Time is the most valuable material in the world, and there at least we all start equally, but I was taught to scatter mine thoughtlessly, as though it were infinite. Now for the first time I feel morally and mentally free, and yet they say there is no freedom here. If a paper pass or an identification card hampers one's freedom, then it is true. There may be restrictions to the individual and if I were a Russian subject I might not be allowed to leave the country, but I seem to have been obliged to leave England rather clandestinely!!

Freedom is an illusion. There really is not any in the world, only the freedom one creates intellectually for one's self.

My work is ended, but I am loath to go. I love this place. I love the people who pass by me in the street. I love the atmosphere laden with melancholy, with sacrifice, with tragedy. I am inspired by this Nation purified by Fire. I admire the dignity of their suffering and the courage of their belief.

I would like to live among them forever, or else work for them outside; work and fight for the Peace that will heal their wounds.

NOVEMBER 5TH 1920. Moscow.

A message has arrived third hand from Kalinin offering to sit to me. He promised to a long time ago, before he went to the front. He got back from the front on October 30th with Kamenev, and had he given me the chance then there would have been plenty of time. Now everything is settled for me to go to-morrow with Professor Lomonosoff in his special train. I am very disappointed. Kalinin has a head that interests me.

I have wanted to do a Russian peasant type, and he is one. But if I don't get away in Lomonosoff's train I may delay a long time. England seems so very far away, and the children think I have forgotten them. Perhaps if I could work without my fingers getting frozen I would stop and do him, and do Litvinoff too. But I have made a failure of my soldier, and it is not encouraging. An appointment was made for me with Kalinin at I o'clock to see him in his office. Litvinoff kindly took me there. It was in some building facing the Kremlin. We went in and after some searching, and enquiry, found the outer rooms of his office. There seemed to be two or three of these, and they were full of people sitting on benches round the wall. Some looked miserable, and were curled up in a heap with shawls over their heads, others were sleeping in corners, or huddled up by the stove. They spat on the floor, smoked and were perfectly silent. These were all people who came with a grievance to lay before their President. Litvinoff when he went in asked whether it was Kalinin's office—a nod and a grunt assented that it was. Litvinoff, who is impatient, went from room to room, but we could find no trace of Kalinin. Finally he opened a door that proved to be the private office. A short haired girl secretary looked up and said Kalinin might come in half an hour. So he might, but with an experience of Russian official appointments, it seemed likely that he might not appear for a couple of hours. We left messages and retreated.

On our way out some one, rousing himself from a corner, asked whether Kalinin was really in his room or not. Perhaps they thought we were privileged people, while they were kept waiting. I was rather glad that we could say he was not there. I came away with a melancholy impression of the place, but Kalinin with his kindly face, must be the best sort of man to whom the people can tell their troubles.

We then drove to the statue of Dostoyevski, which is a beautiful bit of work in granite that I wanted to photograph. In the same square there is another granite statue by the same artist, which is usually known as "The Thinker." It is if anything better than the Dostoyevski.

From there I went to the Kremlin to see how the packing of my heads was progressing. I was surprised to find that the wooden cases had been delivered, owing, no doubt, to the combined efforts of Kamenev, Litvinoff, Andreef and my kind Comrad Ynachidse, from whom all blessings flow.

Moreover, the heads were packed, there was nothing for me to do. I said good-by very sadly to my nice moulder whom I like so much. He is intelligent, well-mannered, and efficient. He bent down and kissed my hand with the simplicity and dignity of a prince. I gave him a woolen jersey, as he feels the cold, and with all his thousands of roubles that he earns he cannot buy such a thing.

I gave one last look round the grim room to which I have become attached, and with a lump in my throat departed down the long stone passage through which my footsteps reechoed for the last time.

Then I crossed the courtyard and went to lunch at the Kremlin table d'hôte. This table d'hôte, which is the Communist restaurant reserved for all the Commissars and workers in the Kremlin, was unusually full to-day. I was lucky to get a place. Lunarcharsky sat opposite me. He has just returned to Moscow and I regret there was no one present who could introduce us.

My neighbors observed me reading an English guide book to the Kremlin, and attempted odd bits of conversation, but their English completely broke down. It is a great loss not being able to understand a word of Russian, as the general conversation at the long table was very animated and must have been interesting.

The interest for me was in the faces of the men themselves, who were of the most varied types it would be possible to collect. One could not say they were typically Russian or typical of any race or of any particular character, and yet there was some invisible link that bound all these men together in one common thought.

After lunch Andreef fetched me and an official showed us all over the Tsar's Palace. There were exquisite small rooms with vaulted ceilings and frescoed walls, from which it was evident the stage scenery in the Russian operas had been copied. There were still traces of red bunting and appeals to the workers of the world to unite, in the colossal room over-decorated with gold, which was the Throne Room of the Romanoffs, and in which the Third International had its last meeting place.

The modern apartments in the new wing are bad architecture and bad taste, but everything is left undisturbed. Even the photographs of the Tsar's Coronation are still hanging in their frames in some of the rooms. The Royal Family scarcely came to Moscow, so the place must have always had an uninhabited feeling. One did not feel the ghosts of former times as in some of the older parts of the building.

My last evening was spent with Andreef, Litvinoff, and Kamenev, who came and sat in my room.

Kamenev brought me a sheepskin hat, such as I had seen at the Zuckarefski market, and wanted so much. Also the 100 I had entrusted to his care when we started, which I have never had occasion to spend. He then told me that my departure is most ill-timed. To-morrow is the eve of the Anniversary of the Revolution. There are going to be great celebrations. A big meeting will be held at the opera house, at which Lenin and Trotsky are going to speak. It is only on very rare occasions that Lenin appears in public, and it would be interesting to hear him. The meeting is called for 4 o'clock, but it will be 3 or 4 hours late, and my train leaves at 8. If only Lomonosoff would delay his train I could attend. The next day, on the 7th, there will be a ball, and on the 8th a banquet at our house for the Foreign Office.

Moreover the Entente papers promise a coup d'etat for the 7th and Litvinoff suggested that I should wait and "see the show." But I know by experience that I would only wait in vain. When I was alone with Kamenev he said to me: "Well, did I keep my promises?" I told him that everything had been fulfilled, and had exceeded even my expectations. I told him I was overwhelmed by the kindness I had received, "considering I am an enemy Englishwoman." He would not listen to any words of appreciation. He smiled in his genial kindly way: "of course we were glad to receive you, and to have you among us, une femme artiste—what did it matter to us, your nationality, or your relations. There is only one thing que nous ne pouvons pas supporter [we cannot stand]"—and for the first time in all the months I have known him a hard look passed over his face and he set his teeth:

"The only thing we cannot stand, c'est l'espionage," and the way he said it gave me a shiver down my spine. It was only a passing shadow, and the next moment he was telling me he really regarded me as a woman of courage for coming just on his word, adding that when he saw me on the departure platform "with two small hand bags, I knew in that moment that you were not any ordinary woman!" We looked back on our London days and laughingly discussed the first sitting when he invited me to come to Moscow. I told him, "I did not believe you were serious when you asked me!" And he said, "Neither did I believe you were serious when you accepted!" He then proceeded to outline for me exactly what the effect of my Moscow visit would have on my friends, on my family, in the press, and on my career. His accuracy remains to be seen.

NOVEMBER 6TH, Saturday.

Off at last what a hectic day. Litvinoff telephoned to me in the morning from the Commissariat to say that my big wooden cases (my coffins I call them, they are the same shape) were going to be conveyed from my studio to the station, and that I need not concern myself about them. It was not until midday that I learnt for certain that Professor Lomonosoff was going to start to-night.

In Russia one makes no plans, things happen when they happen! With a rashness that nearly proved reckless, I distributed my few belongings among my friends. To a lady doctor friend of Andreef who had been nice to me, I left all my stockings, a box of soap, a skirt, a jersey and my cloth overcoat. To the maids in the house, my shoes and isseds, workbag, jersey, fur-lined dressing jacket, pair of gloves, and hat. To Rothstein as a parting gift, my hotwater bottle and medicine case. I started on my journey with the clothes I stood up in. The maids, to my intense embarrassment, kissed my hands and nearly wept. I nearly kissed them in return. I started off with Litvinoff, and Rothstein came to the front door to see the last of me. He overwhelmed me with compliments: "You have been a brick, you have played up splendidly, you have never complained" I tried to explain that I hadn't played up, and I hadn't been anything except very happy.

I might have added that living Communistically had proved to me that one must either love or hate the people one sees everyday for any length of time. Hate may be tempered into dislike, and Love may be more appropriately friendship or affection, but it, was certainly affection that I had grown to feel for Rothstein. He seemed somehow to belong to our environment,—we should have missed him if he hadn't been there. Just occasionally he said things about England that roused opposition in me. I feel about England as most people do about their relations, that I may abuse my own, but no one else may 1 I realized when I got to know him better that his attitude was not so much one of hostility to England, as of intense pride in Russia, and so I forgave him!

During my first days in Moscow Rothstein unfailingly cross-questioned me at supper, as to how I had spent my day, where I had lunched, who I'd seen, and what time I had come home. At last I said to him: "Don't ask me, try and find out " and I chaffed him so that he had to give up asking. I never knew whether there was a motive in his curiosity or not. At all events, he never was anything but a kindly and helpful friend to me. I drove away from No. 14 Sofiskaya Naberezhnaya in an open car in the bright light of a full moon, glittering stars and hard frost. Litvinoff, observing that I looked back at it rather sentimentally said: "That is your Moscow home, the next time you come you will bring your children," and I felt that I did not look upon it for the last time. We drove first to the Commissariat for Foreign Affairs, as he had some packages of papers to pick up there which he had taken away in the morning to have sealed up for me. I waited outside in the car for some time. When he rejoined me he was agitated. My "coffins" he had just learnt were still at the Kremlin. Organization had miscarried, it was "somebody's" fault. The lorry had waited for them 3 hours, the sentry at the building had refused to deliver up the cases. What could have happened? Every one was at the big Opera House meeting, so all telephoning efforts to get hold of responsible help had been in vain. We had three-quarters of an hour before the train was due to start. I suggested driving to the Kremlin to see what we could do. Happily I still had my pass on me, so we got in, by the sentry. The building, ever before so busy, was now utterly deserted and resonant. I unlocked the door of my studio,—there were the two coffins lying packed and sealed and unmoved. I lifted one end of one, it was far beyond our combined strengths to carry, and the motor could not have taken them. We gave it up in despair. Down in the courtyard our car refused to move, the chauffeur was tinkering at it. It seemed to have a real congested chill.

Train time was drawing near. The station was some way off. "Stay," said Litvinoff. I had visions of staying, perhaps indefinitely, having parted with all except what I stood in.

I looked round at the beautiful Kremlin, to which I had already said good-by, not expecting to see it again. It seemed more beautiful than ever, more still, more dignified, more impassive.

The clock in the old Spassky tower complainingly chimed three times, it was a quarter to seven. At last the car breathed, pulsed, started, then stopped. Then pulsed, grunted, and started again.

We were off, and as the road lay downhill, it seemed possible the car, which was missing badly, might get there! It seemed to be an evening of mishaps, and I felt fated not to leave Moscow.

However, we reached the station at exactly seven and I gathered up all I could in each hand, and ran towards a crowd that stood by the only train in the station. Litvinoff shouted to me, "You needn't run." Indeed, I need not, the only train in the station was not the train of Professor Lomonosoff. His special came in at another platform about half an hour later, and never went out till after 9. Had we known, something could have been done in the time to get the cases to the train, also I could have gone to the meeting and heard Lenin. No one was more frantic than Lomonosoff himself, who prided himself on his train being punctual. But it could not be helped, the train had just returned from the Urals, and was in a state of disorder!

Litvinoff, when he said good-by to me, promised to send on my cases by courier to Reval in time to catch the Stockholm boat. He then roused my curiosity by telling me that he had been a better friend to me than I should ever know. I begged him to explain, but he said I must wait ten years or so.

NOVEMBER 7TH, 1920. In the train.

Professor Lomonosoff is the Minister of Railways. We are carrying six and a half million pounds in gold, which he is taking to Germany to buy locomotives with. We are accompanied by an armed guard.

We were held up many hours last night because there was an accident on the line and it took a long time to clear. Periodically the axle of the gold car breaks, or the oil-box takes fire, and we stop perpetually: but we are steadily nearing our goal. It really does not matter how long we take so long as we catch next Thursday's boat from Reval.

Our party consists besides Lomonosoff's staff, which he is taking with him to Germany, of Vanderlip and Neuorteva, and a charming man called Dargone, who is a railway expert. He was once a very rich man and in the Tsar's entourage. He seemed anxious to 'tell me as quickly as possible that he was a Monarchist, as if to be mistaken for a Bolshevik were more than he could bear.

He looked anaemic and well bred, with deep-set sad eyes and a calm and resignation that were almost tragic.

He differed bitterly and openly in his views from Lomonosoff and said, "I am a Russian. I am working for Russia, not for the Bolsheviks," whom he called robbers! Professor Lomonosoff sat back in his chair and chuckled. He said: "You call us robbers, but we called you robbers." It was just a question of which robber came out top.

Afterwards when Lomonosoff left us, I begged D—not to indulge in any more political discussions. "I shall be over the frontier in a few hours, but you have to live here. Do take heed for yourself."

He shrugged his shoulders. "One dies but once," he said, laughing, and then explained:

"They know my views well; but I can do good work for them, and they know I am not in touch with counter-revolutionary movements, and that I take no part in politics, so I am safe enough."

Lomonosoff, who had been a railway official in Tsarist days, told us how he had accompanied the Tsar's train to Tsarskoe-Selo. The Tsar, he said, had even up to that moment not realized the meaning of the Revolution. He probably thought he was retiring to Siberia until the storm had blown over. At the station, upon his arrival, his bodyguard had by courtesy been drawn to greet him.

The Tsar alighted from the train and went to inspect the guard with the usual greeting: "Good health to you soldiers!" The answer is: "Good health to your Imperial Majesty," but on this occasion the soldiers answered almost in one voice.

"Good health to you, Colonel!" The Tsar seemed to realize for the first time the real situation. He became ashen white, turned the collar of his overcoat up, and shrank away.

Lomonosoff also gave us a vivid and thrilling account of the detailed organization, in which he took part, with the purpose of wrecking the Tsar's train while he was on his way to Siberia.

Two runaway engines were to be despatched, with no one on board, to collide with the back of the Tsar's train. These plans were only frustrated at the last second by the news of the Tsar's abdication.

When he proceeded to tell us how the Tsar's entourage deserted him as rats do a sinking ship, it was evidently very painful to Dargone, who sat grimly silent. I could not help feeling that they a little bit enjoyed his discomfiture.

Later, when we were again alone together, he said to me rather passionately, "It is not true that every one deserted my Tsar, for my best friend followed him to Siberia to share his death, and there were devoted friends of the Tsaritza who did the same."

We are now nearing the frontier. The little country stations decorated for the 7th with red bunting and pictures of Lenin will soon be passed.

Back we go to the old world of tips and restaurants, and civilization.

Good-by, wonder world, good-by—good-by!

NOVEMBER 12TH, 1920.

We arrived in Reval late on Tuesday night the 9th. I was handed a package containing my two volumes of diary and all my Kodak films, which, thanks to Litvinoff, had been sealed with Government seals and confided to a courier who kept them in his charge until we were over the frontier.

I have written my diary all these weeks as trustingly as though I were in my own home, never foreseeing any difficulties of departure. My trust in Providence is always justified.

The next day I went to the British Consulate.

Mr. Leslie (no relation) made me extremely welcome. He said he had heard of me from H. G. Wells, and that until then he had not known I was in Russia. I had (reproachfully) not addressed myself to the Consulate on my in-going journey. I found he had a Henry James cult, and had read everything Henry James had written, including the two volumes of letters. He gave me his bath-room for an hour and a half, invited me to luncheon and then arranged for me to stay the remaining two days in Reval with a most hospitable

English couple, Mr. and Mrs. Harwood, who lived in a beautiful villa on the seashore. There I was overwhelmed by kindness.

I also learned with some curiosity and interest the politics of Esthonia, the half Bolshevist condition of things, and the history of the Baltic Germans, their settlement in Reval and their forced departure. It is an amusing and complicated little side-show.

During my stay in Reval I had to go several times to the Soviet headquarters at the Hotel Petersbourg. It amuses me to recall my bewildered impression of last September. This time when I went I felt thoroughly at home! Not only did Comrad Gai take a great deal of trouble for me, but Gukofski received me as a friend.

On Thursday morning the coffins arrived from Moscow, by courier, as promised by Litvinoff, and I had a fine game of dodge. Gai sent them on a lorry to me at the British Consulate, just when I had left, and they returned to the Hotel Petersbourg while I was chasing after them to the British Consulate. Finally I got them down to the quay but they were not allowed on board because there was not the required official paper from Moscow. Had the ship left as she was supposed to leave, at midday, they certainly would not have been on board, but there was a storm brewing so the ship delayed sailing a day. When Gai had finally sent me the necessary paper, I sought out the Captain and begged him to have my cases put somewhere especially safe. "They contain the heads of Lenin and Trotsky," I explained. The Captain looked awfully impressed and pleased, so pleased that I added, "Plaster heads—and breakable."

"A plaster head of Trotsky—and breakable—?

Come on! Let's break Trotsky's head!" and he made towards it threateningly, much to the amusement of the onlookers.

My departure from Reval was superintended by my late Bolshevist hosts, whose representatives in Reval, and also Professor Lomonosoff and his staff, did everything in their power to be kind and attentive.

We are on our way now to Stockholm...I find the same Swedish banker, Mr. Aschberg, on board who went across with us in

September. He is in charge of a cabin full of gold. He takes good care of me and I am glad to find a friend. I am told the food on board is very bad, but I think it is marvelous.

NOVEMBER 1 6TH, 1920.

Have lost all track of time. Storms forced our little boat to anchor under the shelter of an Oland isle for two days and a night.

On our arrival late at night at Stockholm we were met by Professor Lomonosoff's representative with a car, and after we had all been submitted to a search, not for arms, but for insects, and declared fit to step on to Swedish soil, I was whirled off to the Hotel Anglais.

I was fully expected to be lost and forgotten on leaving Moscow, but here I am being taken care of in the third country away. If the Stockholm experiences foreshadow my coming reception in England, it promises to be hectic. I. am not allowed breathing space, nor eating time.

Reporters besiege me. They even walk up to my room without being announced. I am so ignorant of the papers they represent that I say all the wrong things. One paper, a Conservative one, says that I declared Trotsky to be a perfect gentleman. This, if it gets back to Moscow, is most embarrassing. Never in my wildest moments would I use so mediocre a description to apply to Trotsky. I might say he was a genius, a superman, or a devil. Anyway, in Russia we talk of men and women and not of ladies and gentlemen.

I dare say the editor meant well, and things get distorted in translation.

The experience of returning through Stockholm is rather unique. Because we have both come out of Russia together, Mr. Vanderlip and I have been entertained at the same parties, but for me Frederick Strom and the Russian Bolshevists are invited, and for Vanderlip the leading Swedish bankers. It is a queer amalgamation, but it works well.

The first evening I talked to Socialist Strom and a Conservative banker for an hour and a half in flowing but execrable German. They did not laugh at my grammar, and they listened and spurred me on with questions. The German of my childhood slightly practiced in Moscow has returned to me with a rush.

I have been invited to do a monument for a public square in Stockholm representing peace uniting the workers of the Right and Left Wing.

The money has been subscribed in kronor by the workpeople. It is an international thing, and they would be pleased if I would do it. It is a subject which rather lends itself to allegorical treatment and appeals to the imagination.

I am now in the night train for Goteborg. Before I left I went to tea with the children at the Palace. The Crown Prince unfortunately was in Rome. The children seemed lonely, but well.

Princess Ingrid looked sad, big-eyed, and rather I ale. The baby, Johnny, is adorable. He is a thing so sweet to woman, so much to be appreciated. One feels the maternal spirit-arms round him.

I also went to see the Controller of the Queen's household (an artist and an old friend of many years). Here the impression I received of prejudice against my Russian friends was overwhelming, but I suppose in Court circles this is to be expected.

NOVEMBER I8THI 1920.

Goteborg to Newcastle.

More delays, owing to storms. Always there are delays on this journey. Do what one will it is impossible to hurry. In pre-war days it took two days to come from Russia. Now it takes two weeks.

NOVEMBER 23RD, 1920. London.

We arrived at Newcastle at midnight on the

19th. Steaming up the Tyne at night is wonderful, all the arclights throwing into relief great machinery and construction. The activity and work looked colossal. As soon as we had glided alongside the quay, and I had touched English soil once more, I was not left in doubt one moment as to the truth of Kamenev's premonitions.

While the coffins were being opened with chisel and hammer at the Custom House, reporters, who declared they had come from London and had been waiting two days, clamored for information.

The head official of the Customs was very abrupt in his manner and subjected all my luggage to a most ruthless search. I did not declare the' identity of my heads, but from the unpleasant official attitude I guessed they were already known.

One official began examining a large album of photographs. I said to him, "That isn't contraband, it's photographs of my work. Yes, that one is Mr. Churchill,—if it interests you, you may look at it " He nearly flung it down. "I've no scent and no tobacco, one doesn't get those things in Russia" I said. Unfortunately at that minute he came upon a packet of Soviet cigarettes, my last ration that I had carefully kept and brought back to England. But he said, "That's not what we are looking for " Whatever he was looking for he didn't find.

He then poked his arm up to the elbow in the straw and shavings that wrapped up Dsirjinsky, until satisfied that it was not a Xmas bran-pie.

I then got it nailed down again, and accepted the newspaper reporters' invitation to drive with them from the quay to the station. There another man met me armed with a isse and a flashlight. I sympathize with professional keenness but I will not be butchered to make a Roman holiday. The moment seemed inappropriate. There were inebriate young fellows shouting, singing, and falling about the station to such an extent that the policeman, who had vainly tried to look the other way, had finally to take notice, but he had to knock one of them down before he could arrest him. It was a revolting sight and I was glad to get into my sleeper and shut out the sight and sound of Newcastle at midnight.

Since then my soul, my life, my time, has been no longer my own. I have been pursued, besieged, harassed, feasted, attacked, and praised in turn....

I have seen prejudice and hate and bitterness.

Russia, to-day, is a new phenomenon, but the opposition is merely history repeating itself. We read of the same condition of mind in England after the Napoleonic wars; the same fear of French Revolutionary ideas, the same actions and reactions.

Yet, if people would only realize it, Revolutions are not caused by propaganda, nor by plots. In Russia the Revolution failed every time it was organized. It was brought about, by cause and effect, at the very moment the present leaders were in exile, in the four corners of the globe.

Alexinsky says in his "Modern Russia," "Seek for the cause of Revolution neither in the ardent propaganda of the Revolutionists, nor in the bad qualities of monarchs and their advisers, but in the deep and silent operation of certain forces, which lead new social classes upon the stage of History." It is futile to waste hate upon these forces, or to call them Lenin and Trotsky, when really it is the law of evolution and change that is demonstrating in certain parts of the Earth.

JAN., 1921.

Since my return from Moscow on November

20th, 1920, I have hardly had a breathing space first there were the "Times" publication of my Diary and all it involved, then the writing of my book, which is only just finished.

When I started off to Moscow without a word to any one, I could not surmise what would be the outcome of it, nor what the attitude of my family and friends would be. I have returned to find a revelation of surprises. It is a bitter world,—the world to which I once belonged,—and they do me the compliment of taking me a good deal more seriously than I have ever taken myself. In fact very seriously.

But my adventure has shaken off a good many of those worthless friends with which one gets unavoidably lumbered up as the years go on and one's tastes and ideas evolve. But I have made more new friends than the old ones lost.

And I like my new friends. I talk heart to heart and soul to soul with them. At last, and for the first time, almost, in my life I am among people with whom I talk the same language.

Nearly two months have flashed by, full of incident and interest—impossible to record.

Strange people call on me and ask for me on the telephone—strange only insomuch as they are unknown to me, but not strange for long....

One day Massingham asked me to lunch with him and I went not knowing him. My friend Capt. Grenfell was of the party. I loved Massingham and to this day I think I have enjoyed my talk with him more than any other. Bernard Shaw too I met at dinner at Sidney Cooke's, but Shaw with all his wit and genius has not the fierce flame that is characteristic of the Russian spirit.

Massingham has a bitter sense of humor, and one feels in him the fight of the worker, whereas in Shaw one recognizes the rather "lazy" man, who sees what is wrong, but without its arousing more than a jest and a sardonic hit of the pen at his adversary. Shaw is a man of letters, first and foremost. Massingham is concerned with bettering the world. I believe he will fight his hardest, he would go under fighting. He is unbreakable, he has the passion that the Russians have.

He asked me to write something for the "Nation" and I tried, but it is not easy to write an article, whereas it is very easy to write a Diary. An article at once is pretentious and one has to know one's subject in all its aspects. I do not want to tempt Providence by doing something amateurish. My writing is like my modeling—I can do something quick from life, that has the impression and the freshness of perception—to toil at a solid piece of work I am incapable and would fail.

I have been asked by Coates, the Secretary of the "Hands Off Russia Committee," to address big meetings at Liverpool, Bradford, Manchester, etc., but I refused as, however non-political I might be, I would unavoidably be branded by a political platform. He asked me to meet Robert Williams and Malone. Williams is a serious, intent and deep thinking man. Malone is young and new to the game and not big minded enough.

But he has the spirit of sacrifice.

JAN. 14, 1921.

I lunched with Kitty Somerset and found the Bernard Shaws there. Kitty is splendid. Shaw was very entertaining. We had discussions on education, children, religion and so on. We all agreed on the misery of childhood. Shaw says that children have the right to get up and walk away if their teachers bore them! I asked him whether I ought to persist in making my children say prayers every night, when it means no more to them than the bread and milk which accompanies the pre-bed time moment. Ought one not to get away from shams and stick to realities? The table was divided in opinion about this, and Shaw told us that when he was a child he used to improvise his own prayers, and end up with the Lord's Prayer, until suddenly one day out in the sun, he realized that he did not believe in it, and that it was all unnecessary nonsense, and resolved to give it up. The first night, he said, he went to sleep with a feeling of omission and consequent discomfort. After that it was all forgotten. He then proceeded to tell us that all the Jonah and the Whale and such-like tales have the effect of ruining the Christian faith and muddling children's heads—Atheists wipe out everything and consequently start on a clean sheet and end in believing something worth while.

JAN. 15.

Had my passport photos done and Mr. Coates lunched with me. He read me a letter from Rothstein from Moscow, in which Rothstein, who is obviously homesick, nevertheless describes the improvement in the conditions of everything, particularly of food. In fact it made such good reading that I felt my sympathy for my friends in Moscow was no longer required.

After lunch Dick arrived from Honseley and brought me the last news of my beloved Teeta, who is evidently getting on very well.

JAN. 16.

Fitzie gave Dick and me lunch at Caunto's we were late, and Fitzie was walking up and down outside quite cheerfully without any coat or hat on. After lunch we went to the Zoo. I like Fitz's unconventionality and "je m' en fichiste" air. He gave me dinner and came back to the studio afterwards to talk peacefully. We talked about the United States. He returned not very long ago.

He says that one has a wonderful time but that it costs a million a minute to live—and that is the very devil of it for English people. He says I ought not to start off into the unknown with the burden of Dick and that while I am on tour, lecturing, I should not have the fun of seeing him and all the anxiety of wondering how he was getting on.

Of course Fitzie was talking sense. I had sure issed all that to myself long ago, but firmly repressed it. However, the result of our evening was that Fitzie took the tickets away in his pocket to take them to the Cunard office to cancel the two extra ones. I went to bed a very sad woman.

America is only contemplatable with Dick, and if I have to go without him it will be a wretched business.

JAN. 17. Monday.

I sent my passport papers all filled up and signed to Sidney, to the Reform Club, and he is going to deal with the matter for me. There seem to be delays that one suspects of being deliberate—I feel none too easy just yet about that passport.

At quarter to one I arrived at the "Daily Herald" office as directed by Mr. Ewer and met Lansbury, who took us, three others, to lunch somewhere nearby. Ewer then approached me on the subject of doing a head of Lansbury—there is terribly little time, but I said I thought I could do it if Lansbury would sit every day for an hour.

Even that only gives me four days. Lansbury demurred and was shy and had to be talked to severely. Finally he consented. He's got a good head, a very characteristic one, which should not be difficult. I find him easy to talk to, and he seems to love (as I do) to talk over Moscow.

JAN. I 8. Tuesday.

Lansbury sat at 10:30. Lunched with Dennis Trefusis at the I Royal—'while we were lunching Sidney brought me my passport.

After lunch Dennis came with me to the American Consulate, but it was useless as I hadn't the lawyer's letter vouching for my respectability!

What red tape—time is getting short!

At 5 I had tea with the Forbes Robertsons. I am to take care of "Blossom" who is crossing on the flquitania. I stupidly thought of her as I had known her years ago, a lovely child, and I told her mother on the telephone that I would be delighted to take care of her, and that I'd wash her and dress her! Blossom, however, turns out to be grown up!

I have changed my mind about not taking Dick and Louise with me and I rang up Fitzie, who marvelously was not bad tempered at being asked to get the ticket back from Cooks'. He just laughed, and did as I asked him, and cancelled the cancellations. I don't know why I've changed my mind. I just have a blind instinct that I must have Dick on the other side of the ocean. I will trust to luck that he will be taken care of, and Providence never lets me down.

JAN. 19. Wednesday.

Lansbury came punctually at 10:30. He stayed till 12:15, and talked the whole time. I think he likes me and does not find it tedious to "sit" as he expected. Mr. Ewer did not come which shows that he did not mind facing the hours alone with me. We talked a good deal about Moscow, and about Lenin, and we both agreed about Lenin being curiously obstinate in his own views. For instance, nothing that one can tell him about the position in England avails in any way. He persists in his misinformation. Lansbury assured Lenin there was no Revolutionary movement in England that was of any account—but this he simply would not believe. At midday Larisbury rushed away, late for his meeting! A few minutes later Mr. Cousins, the President of the Phrenological Society, arrived and I spent an absorbingly interesting hour with him. He measured the Russian heads as far as it was possible, but unfortunately the measurements that concern me are not thee, measurements that concern him. His interest centers in the back of the head and cranium,—mine of course is with the features and outline of the face. He was, however, able to deduce a good deal, and while he was measuring and observing I took down hasty notes of what he dictated. His summing up of each man was so accurate,—at least it coincided so extraordinarily with the judgment I had formed of them myself, that I accused him of knowing something about them individually. But he assured me he knew nothing whatever beyond the average prejudices shared by the general public.

I confess that I had viewed with some anxiety the report he might make. For instance suppose he had declared sweepingly that they all were criminal lunatics! I should have been terribly disappointed. I felt like some one who goes to a fortune teller, impelled by curiosity, but terrified of what he might hear. It turned out so much better than I expected that I warned Mr.

Cousins his report, if made public, would savor of Bolshevik propaganda, and would recoil (I can now speak feelingly!) on his own head! One thing which had been mystifying me was the fact that three out of the four men I did in Moscow had sloping backs to their heads. The one who apparently had not was Trotsky, but then his hair is so thick that it was difficult to tell whether he also had this characteristic or not. Mr. Cousins explained to me that it meant their powers of concentration and administration outbalanced and counter-balanced their amativeness.

In a letter, Mr. E. W. Cousins, President of the British Phrenological Society, Incorporated, generalizes the characteristics of the leaders from the scientific standpoint. He says: "Education and environment are very important factors affecting the expression of mentality. The present leaders of the Bolsheviks have without exception been in prison or suffered severe punishment on account of their opinions. This treatment must be considered in judging their character. It must affect their mental outlook.

"Considering the exhausted and bleeding condition of the country when they assumed power they were compelled to act swiftly and drastically.

The problems they had to face were tremendous.

"The leaders of the present government are all firm, determined, energetic, hard workers and hard fighters. The softer elements in their nature are kept in the background by the force of circumstances. They are all idealists and their conscientiousness will tend in the direction of their ideals. Any judgment of their character must take these factors into consideration. They have so much business and so little time that they have no room for a patient policy, and obstacles to their schemes have to be swept aside. In this sense they may be cruel and harsh but it is not correct to say that they are cruel and bloodthirsty from a liking or disposition to be such. They can be guilty of severity when in their opinion the conditions demand it, but these men prefer other methods."

Before proceeding with each in detail he summed them up as follows:

Lenin: the statesman.

Trotsky: the military leader.

Zinoviev: the practical administrator.

Dsirjinsky: the aesthete and the philosopher.

Krassin: the business head.

Unfortunately Kamenev's bust had not returned from the foundry, so there was no pronouncement on him at all.

LENIN: His perceptive ability is excellent.

He is able to judge the qualities of things, and his sense of order is good. His reflective power is also large. He is a thinker. Has good planning ability and is systematic. He has great ideals and wishes to do things on a large scale, is benevolent and firm, with great determination.

The religious powers are considerable; their expression will be in the direction prompted by his education and environment. Spirituality appears to be large. He is not particularly anxious to please, but will be more gracious to women than men, unless the men are very closely associated with his ideals and purposes, and pull in the same direction as himself. His intuition does not appear to be relatively strong, and he may sometimes fail properly to appreciate and understand the position of other men. He has considerable driving power and energy. He is secretive, careful and combative. He has a strong sense of his own weight and power and desires everything to contribute to his own purposes and ideals. I can imagine him wishing to sweep away every obstacle that may hinder the progress of his schemes, but he has no pleasure or delight in the means which appear under the present conditions to be essential and right. In other words, his sense of right operates in a direction which he considers to be right.

He is ambitious to achieve. He acquires, not to amass wealth so much as mental gifts and power. He will not easily be moved from his course. His social instincts are good but well under the control of his intellect. He appreciates friends and children and the opposite sex. This latter power controlled by his benevolence, reverence and conscientiousness will cause him to be gracious to women and considerate for their interests.

TROTSKY: His intellect controls his social feelings. Considerable temporal lobe means strong self-preserving instinct. He is cautious, diplomatic and energetic. His whole heart goes into the scheme in hand. He has great perceptive powers and has particular ability to focus and individualize and estimate sizes and weights. A keen sense of place helps him in his military movements. He is critical, original, constructive and analytical. Has excellent planning powers, is very intuitive in practical affairs, will sense as well as plan things. Can be agreeable but is brusque because he is busy. He is firm, determined, idealistic and has large self-esteem. He is right from his own point of view. He wants to do things on a big scale. Has courage and fighting spirit so strong that it swamps his amativeness.

ZINOVIEF: A democratic autocrat, not actuated by his self-esteem, but driven by his ideals.

Has good planning and organizing ability. He is critical, but his fault-finding is toned by human sympathy. A sensualist but controlled. Artistic, courageous, determined, and with a broad outlook and a wide vision. Energetic and ambitious and a fighter. Has less religious feeling than the others. Would have excelled as a musician if he had had time. Has only a fair desire to be agreeable. Intuitive, aggressive and obstinate.

DSIRJINSKY: More theoretical than executive. Moral region less pronounced than in the other men. Efficiency is his great characteristic.

He is exacting, critical, often irritable and suffers from liver.

Great powers of expression; active and energetic mentally and physically, but especially mentally. This man supplies what the others have not; excellent reflective powers. Ascetic, idealistic, philosophical, theoretical, analytical and constructive in the mental line. Great literary powers. Exacting on every one but more exacting on himself. Has benevolence and veneration. Dominated by the intellectual. Enthusiastic, appreciates the beautiful, the grand, the sublime.

KRASSIN: Fine perceptive power. Keen sense of qualities of things and details. Has good reflective powers, has practical common sense, a keen sense of values, is diplomatic, and has practical intuition. Good powers of expression and knows what he wants, and is determined to achieve his ends. Is considerably endowed with social instincts, has a good consciousness of his own ability and has ambition. He is friendly and appreciates children.

ALL are idealistic, determined and courageous and forceful. They are all rather disgruntled men, who have suffered imprisonment, which has poisoned their outlook. They are dissatisfied with the present state of things and determined to force their ideals on others.

In the afternoon I went with Sidney to the U. S.

Consulate, armed with the necessary letter. A good looking gray-haired young man looked at me critically and invited me to "leave" my passport and call for it on Saturday morning. I explained my ship sailed on Saturday! He promised to have it especially seen to immediately—that is "as soon as possible"—evidently there was a hitch. There seemed little enough time for hitches. Later in the day, he telephoned and made an appointment for me to see the consul himself, Mr. Skinner, at

1.0 A. M.

JAN. 20. Thursday.

Papa met me at the Consulate. Mr. Skinner was extremely polite and showed a desire to help, but was very non-committal as to his own powers, or any one else's. After a lot of talk and questioning, I said to him:

"It seems to me more difficult to get into the States than into Russia—" He smiled grimly and said: "Yes, it's hard to get into the Kingdom of Heaven." I went away with no hope, and no despair. He had promised nothing and counseled nothing. I expected a telephone call all day but none came.

JAN. 2I. Friday.

The early morning post brought me a letter from the Consul, advising me to cancel my berths on the Aquitania as he did not expect to be able to do anything in time for me to get off Saturday.

Accordingly I rang up Papa and he offered to go immediately to the Cunard Company and see what he could do. I telegraphed to Willie Wavertree at Horseley so that he should not bring Margaret* and Rosemary to the ship to see me off. Then I reflected on the situation sadly but philosophically.

Everything that happens to me, that is not of my own planning, always turns out for the best. I have never believed that I am the arbiter of my own fate,—so I accepted the position and not without curiosity and interest prepared to await developments. The only evils that I could see were, 1st, the possibility that I might have to forfeit the journey money (no joke) and 2nd, that if the U. S.

definitely refused me a vise, I might find an equal difficulty if I tried France or Italy, as all these governments copy one another. The prospect of being marooned in England, with the odd possibility of being perhaps allowed to enter Russia, was rather deplorable and I wrote, in the heat of the moment, a rather disconnected letter to Mrs. Litvinoff, in which I deplored Bolshevism and all it involved, and said something about not having received one single letter from Moscow since my departure.

At 10:30 Lansbury came to sit, soon followed by Ewer. I was in the act of explaining to them that everything had been cancelled when the telephone rang and Mr. Skinner, the Consul, informed me that all was clear, and if I would come down with my passports immediately he would put them right for me. It was a dramatic moment. Lansbury got down from the model stand and said to me, "go at once" and assured me I could not work in such circumstances—he was very kind and considerate, and I let him go with regret. I have made quite a good start with him. However, then came another telephone,—it was Peter.

He offered to go immediately to the Cunard Company and see if he could stop the transfer of my ticket. (The Cunard Company must think me mad.) Willie had to be re-telegraphed to—the Consulate had to be reached immediately. While the passport was being viseed, a consular official observed: "What is against you, Mrs. Sheridan, is that you were not put in prison when you were in Moscow." So that is the trouble!

Loulou Harcourt came to lunch and after lunch my friends turned up en masse—Aunt Leonie Leslie first, with Mary Crawsbray and Priscilla Annesley and Freddy Dufferin—to be succeeded by Madame Krassin, Bob Williams, Ewer, Francis Meynell, Coates and Mrs. Coates, Captain Grenfell, and into it came hurtling Oswald Birley and Hazel Lavery with a young man who had just returned from Hungary and was interesting. What an afternoon! And then, having not yet packed a mortal thing, I went and dined at Aunt Jennie's, a family farewell party. It was late when I got back to the studio and later still when I turned in. Three hours sleep I had before I caught my train.

JAN. 22, 1921.

At 8 A. M. I found an unexpectedly large proportion of my family at the station. It was very creditable!

Aunt Jennie and Porch, Aunt Leonie and Papa, all turned up in plenty of time and looking nearly cheerful. Oswald Birley also came, and just as the train was about to start he found a friend of his, MacDermot, whom he quickly introduced.

Blossom Forbes Robertson was handed over to my care by her father. Mamma said good-by as she always says "goodnight" as if I really was going to America! Peter came along with us to Liverpool. I was terribly sleepy, having only slept three hours, and whenever my eyes closed Dick sat on me or fell on me, or threw something at me, or laughed or cried or romped with Peter.

When we arrived at a view of the ship and Dick saw the four orange funnels, he shouted and clapped his hands and stroked my face and said:

"Thank you, Mema, for taking me with you!

Oh, thank you!" On board we found Margaret waiting for me in my cabin, and we joined Willie and Rosemary who were lunching in the saloon.

Margaret looked lovely but pale and big eyed.

It was a joy to see her up and dancing and running once more, instead of the little serious weak girl I left in bed after appendicitis. She starts for Cannes to join Sophie* on the 19th which will be Heaven for her, but she hated not coming with us and how I hated leaving her. When the gongs sounded f6r the visitors to go ashore, we seemed to renew those painful school-day partings, but I think this time she was the one who did not cry.

'JAN. 28. Saturday. On the eve of arrival.

In 1910 I went for the first and only time to America, and I remember, then, as now, I was perhaps the only soul on board who regretted the journey's end. When on the final morning, New York, like a great imaginary dream city, arose towers high from out of the sea, every one got excited and restless, and conjectured how soon they would be able to leave the ship. I alone looked on calmly and wonderingly and with the curious sensation that to leave the ship would be a sort of uprooting. This time exactly the same process is evolving within me. I always take root anywhere in a week (unless the place is unusually uncongenial). I love the sea, and the sound of the sea, and the big ship has become like a little world. One has sifted out the congenial spirits, and the rest don't count except just as population.

It is a motley crowd. There are besides the British and the American, French, Russian, Spanish, Italian, Japanese and Chinese. There is no international spirit among us. Only the British and Americans seem to dovetail. The French keep exclusively to themselves, so do the Spaniards.

As for the Japanese, they speak to none, and no one speaks to them.

Lopokova is on board, the wonderful little Russian dancer, who ruined the Russian ballet in London when she ran away and was lost. She was a delight in the "Bontique Fantasque," and quite irreplaceable. She has the sad wistful Russian face, that has become familiar to me. I see her standing sometimes a frail little figure and all alone, looking over the ship's side, and I wonder what she is thinking of so distantly.

One of the Orientals dared to ask if he might speak to her. She looked at him with that impassive Russian dignity and shook her head.

"You are Japanese" but he corrected her,—he was Chinese. Her manner changed at once: "Ah, that is delightful," and they talked together for some time. Commander Koehler introduced us.

He is an American naval officer, attached to the State Department, who has spent the last year in Russia, of course on the Wrangel side.

Through him I also met Petchkoff, the adopted son of Gorky, who is also on his way to lecture in America upon "the world as he sees it." If there are any Russians or any one in any way connected with

Russia anywhere near, I always meet them. And I am happy to talk about Russia, and to talk to Russians. The more different their political opinions, the better.

Sir Philip Gibbs is of our company. He is going to lecture on "The Condition of Europe"

Poor America! She's going to get it from every point of view. I wonder what conclusions will result in their minds! Sir Ernest Shackleton, who contemplates another and third Polar expedition, gave us a very good lecture one evening.

It seems as though the Polar earth were his whole life and being. As if there was nothing else for him. It is an obsession. Before I knew he was intent on a third expedition, I remarked on his broad back as he paced the deck. "That is the back of a man who is determined to get there,"

I said, and perhaps he will, next time. From him and from Philip Gibbs and Petchkoff, all of whom have lectured before, I get a lot of information, some of which daunts me. Gibbs says one must have great courage. But Petchkoff says there is no such thing as courage in the world. There is cowardice, but courage is really superfluous energy which is generated by any one of intelligence and good health!

Mr. Marsh, the American who rents Warwick Castle, had letters from Papa and from Fitzie, asking him to seek me out and take special care of me. But Commander Koehler and Frank Mac-

Dermot are the two who have taken upon themselves this burden. Commander Koehler, so far as I am concerned, is an experienced and invaluable adviser. With his help I may steer clear of pitfalls and the inevitable snags of the unwary ignorant!

Whenever I am in greatest need of a friend, some one falls metaphorically from the skies. It happened in Moscow, it is happening again. Providence seems to send me care-takers. Koehler isr of White Russia, but he is one of those rare people who has' a wide horizon and some understanding, whereas Mr. Marsh was instinctively hostile and prejudiced (in spite of Fitz's letter!!).

Koehler placed me at once, he did not attack, he questioned and then assisted. I gave him the MSS. Of my book to read, and he generously admitted that it could not be demanded of me that I should tell other than the truth.—This I have done in my Diary—day by day—as things happened, and not colored by after reflections and opinions. He even says that it would be a pity if I risked blurring my impressions of the men I went to portray by discussions of people of opposite views, of whom I saw much less.

Meanwhile there are conflicting views on board.

Some say I will not be allowed to lecture (no one has tried to find out what I mean to say!), yet others that I will not be allowed to land. All of which leaves me amused but quite unmoved. I know, of course, that this is all absurd,—possibly some sort of a practical joke.—So I answer in kind:

"If I may not lecture it may even come as a great relief. If I may not land, how interesting I shall see Ellis Island,—as a compensation for missing the inside of a Bolshevik prison. But if I do lecture I mean to say what I please. I am the freest woman in the world and of no party.

And the only value of life is in liberty."

We have had a last evening dinner, MacDermot and I arranged it together. The party consisted of Admiral Huse, Commander Koehler, Philip Gibbs and Petchkoff, Blossom, Miss Whyte and Lopokova. The Admiral, who has come into our party at this last, so very late, moment is a charming man. I am lost in admiration of his tact and diplomacy. I have observed on several occasions that he has said the right thing to the right person. For instance he introduced himself to Petchkoff and alluded to his tweed suit as the most distinguished uniform, because of its empty sleeve.

At dinner, the headwaiter, a man who looked like Admiral Beatty, and had a breastful of decorations, asked the Admiral what liqueur he would like. The Admiral looked at him and then at his row of ribbons. One was France

1915—one was Salisbury Plain 1914—the first was South Africa.

140

"This is rather an anti-climax," the Admiral said. "You and I are about equal on that (pointing to the decorations) and then you ask me what liqueurs I'll have!" It showed so much heart and such fine feeling and gave such pleasure—I do admire people who can do those things well.

JAN. 30. Sunday. New York.

At 6 A. M. we were waked by bugles so there was not a chance of remaining in one's bed sleeping! At 7:30 we had to pass the doctor, then Admiral Huse and Commander Koehler joined our table for breakfast.

A horrible morning, raining and cold, one might have been landing in England.

Little Lopokova and I stood hand in hand in the queue which had to pass the passport official.

It took time. So many silly people on board had predicted that I should have difficulties that Koehler promised to be at my side in case of need.

He was amazingly kind and put up with infinite boredom and endless waiting on our accounts. I got clear immediately without the faintest hitch, the rest of the day was spent among pressmen, and at one moment on the upper deck I was made to face a steady row of some dozen kodaks and movie machines. I made Dick come with me, but I felt terribly ridiculous when Koehler's face appeared in the companionway. I felt like sinking through the floor, but he just laughed and understood and was helpful.

During lunch Mr. Lee Keedick appeared and introduced himself. I was most agreeably surprised. I had feared some one rather pushing and unreasonable, but he was extremely nice, human and sympathetic! At his instigation I spent a long time over coffee, giving an interview to the New York "Times" representative. The New York "Times" is a sort of god parent to me, as it published a part of my Diary, but the representative seemed to me an utterly cold human machine.

It was like talking to some soulless thing; one got no response. He never smiled and looked dissatisfied all the way through. I worked very hard it seemed to me, and I thought with no response.*

On shore, at last. Towards 3:30 it was pandemonium, but I got through the customs with the least possible trouble, owing to three or four gallant men, one of the Cunard Line, who took me in charge. It was a moment when I needed help.

And I certainly found it. Koehler was heaven-sent. He just took charge of Dick, took him back to the ship to be out of the hurly-burly, and Dick, who has developed the mad passion of a small man child for a large mature man., went off with him in delight. Again, it is impossible to describe what I feel of gratitude for the patience and kindness of my friends.

Finally a large party of us drove off to the Britmore hotel and Koehler took Dick off my hands until evening, while I with wooly and weary mind talked as amiably and as intelligently as the occasion permitted, to four men at tea time! Mr. Keedick had a secretary waiting for me and she seems splendid and capable. She is to go on tour with me. It is a great help. At 8 I got clear and Koehler took me to dine at the Ritz and then we were able to talk peacefully for the first time in the long eventful day. He was delighted with Dick who seems to have made intelligent remarks about New York which amused him. One of his questions was, why were there no chimney pots on top of the skyscrapers. Why indeed? Now I come to think of it! He loved the lighted-up advertisements and said they help to light the streets!

He brought me home after 11 P. M. The sentinel chaperones who are seated behind desks that are like machine guns placed in commanding positions at the end of each corridor gave one a wicked feeling of guilt. One has the impression that these severe ladies with their ledgers, who observe one's every going in and coming out, are recording opposite to the number of the room, who went in, at what time, and the length of stay.

Koehler left to catch a midnight train for Washington,—how wicked, how adventurous, how devilish one feels with the consciousness of the watchers outside the door! Trotsky's sentinel with fixed bayonet was nothing in comparison—besides, he did not rouse the same curious contrary and self-conscious feelings in me. A sentinel woman is a terrible thing, and a ledger is a worse weapon than a bayonet.

JAN. 31, Monday. Biltmore Hotel.

I feel as if I had been here weeks! Although I have not left my room so many people have passed through it. I have been photographed and given interviews all day. The weariness is in trying not to be indiscreet. It will become second nature to me soon to be cautious! How unlike me.

As for Russia, I am weary of saying what I think about it! But I feel encouraged. My patience and my civility is not in vain. The New York "Times" representative whom I thought so cold and unresponsive has written a most charming account of his interview with me. It is accurate, in good taste and absolutely in the right spirit. But I am no longer free in body and soul.

I have to do what I am told by Mr. Lee Keedick.

It is very odd. I am so surprised at myself, that I feel as if I were outside and looking on at myself with dispassion and amusement. How long will this curious situation last and what will it lead to in the end—?

I am to make my first lecture next Friday here in New York. Mon Dieu! Mon Dieu! What a funny thing for me to be going to do.

At six this evening John Spargo came to see me. This was informal. I really did not know much about him, but I ought to. He is, or was, the leading Socialist here. He is an Englishman.

He knows the Bolshevik leaders and gave me a copy of his book called "The Greatest Failure in all History." It would be interesting to get the Moscow view of him! How they must hate him.

Dick insisted we should accompany him down to the "playroom" which is the room full of toys, a sort of Heaven-Nursery provided by the hotel.

They both slid down the sliding plank! John Spargo was intensely interesting in his analysis of Lenin and Trotsky. He is rather disillusioning about Lenin. In his estimation Lenin is not even a thinker. He says that Lenin is merely a primitive mind. He said that Tolstoi was the same.

It was an illusion to think of him as a thinker.

It was "complex Europe trying to understand the primitive mind," he said. Trotsky he referred to as "a whirlwind among dry leaves." He thought that any one with fire and force like Trotsky could create an army and enthuse the Slav dull minds!

Here where there is education, energy and common sense thought, Trotsky "cut no ice." He agreed, however, with my assertion that Trotsky has developed and evolved with his position since he went away from here.

I wasn't in the least influenced by what John Spargo said, but I was deeply interested in the way he said it. His remarks are crisp and illustrative.

Later.

I have not yet got my bearings nor do I understand the psychology of New York. I am worn out going from place to place that I am asked to, and my odd spare moments are spent in writing little social notes of thanks or refusal. The telephone never stops. America is known worldwide for its hospitality and its genius for entertaining. Nevertheless, I 'feel rather lonely in a big busy prosperous world. I go to parties where there are so many people that I come away as I arrived, a perfect stranger. Names mean nothing to me, and it is impassible to remember so many faces.

America offers one so much food, but will it offer one work? I have never been so unproductively busy. Sometimes I forget that I have not come to America for a spree. In time I shall settle down and sift out my friends. Until then I drift along ignorantly. It is bewildering but interesting. On account of my family, I am in touch with the social side of New York. Through my profession I belong to the artists. On account of my Russian adventure, I am beset by every kind of political current. I feel as if I were in a rudderless boat, wind tossed, at the mercy of tide and storm. Had I a friend, knowledgable, and farseeing, who cared enough, I could be steered carefully. As things are, I must be my own "look-out." But difficulties add to the zest of Life. Endeavoring to overcome difficulties is like battling up hill against the wind on an autumn day. One comes out of it with a sense of health and glow.

"For I know that good is coming to me, that good is always coming—" is the quotation I chalked up on the black wall of my studio years ago. And it has proved true. The words are indelible in my mind and in my heart. But there are moments when I feel as I did in Moscow, that however kind people are, one really stands quite alone.

THE END

BIG BYTE BOOKS is your source for great lost history!

Made in the USA
Las Vegas, NV
09 November 2023

80540283R00088